Bro. Billie Heriford

Greatest pastor
Missouri has ever known

**"With God all things are possible but without Him
no man can achieve God's purpose."**
Apostle Paul

This is an update to a previous book.

This book is dedicated to
A wonderful family,
A good Christian mother
And a father dedicated to being led
By the power and Spirit of God

ISBN978-0-6151-7047-3

Contents

Phase I
The Beginning

Once upon a time, March 18, 1925, to be exact, a little boy was born to Audra Gladys and William (Billie) Heriford. The Herifords already had twin daughters born 17 months before and they condoned the presence of a new one in the family. Billie Heriford, was a young and upcoming preacher. He had just finished practicing his next sermon before the cows, when he was called in for the new emergency. This all took place in a small rural community three miles south of Princeton, Missouri near what was known as the Old Pine church and cemetery. My parents and grandparents and many other relatives are buried there. I will never forget the meetings we attended there and all the relatives that were regular members. The Masons were the mainstay of the church and related by marriage to an Aunt. Little Billy Mason was always there to fire up the old potbelly stove and clean the church. My great-grandmother Nordyke was the Spirit there and I will never forget her Prayers.

Audra Gladys Power Heriford was originally a Kansas Girl but her father, Dow Power, a live stock farmer was forced to move after a large snow storm buried his live stock and he and his wife Mary Picket Power and family moved to the Princeton area. William James Heriford was born to Isaac Vinson and Ethel Nordyke Heriford in the Princeton area. He was one of several in the family and two others were also pastors. The first born of Audra and Billie Heriford, were twins born in Darlington, Missouri on the 27th of November 1923, Martha and Mary to be exact.

Billie began his preaching near Princeton but pastored several churches in northwest Missouri including Darlington, Pattonsberg, King City, Union Star, Maysville and Clarksdale. His ministry was based on the power and grace of God because salaries of that day amounted to what the congregation could bring from their gardens. Imagination would often serve as the staple at mealtime and it was somehow always sufficient to sustain the family. Billie Heriford was not an educated man as some consider education but with a third or four grade education and many hours studying the Bible he attained a superior education for what God had for him to do.

The third year for J.R. took place in Maysville and not many memories can be collected from there. I do remember being called down from a tree when mother almost cried for her little boy. Then again I remember the old coal and wood furnace in the basement but the register was in the center of the door between the living room and dinning room. Martha was not bad, just a little questioning. She discovered that when a kitchen knife was dropped into the furnace it made a nice sound. That of course was not what dad appreciated, as he had to hang head first down in the furnace to retrieve the silverware. I believe while we lived there we had gone to visit friends and as the women were cooking dinner I noticed the stove poker in the wrong place. I knew it should be on the stove and not under the window. I remember pulling it out but I don't remember what happened after that. When I returned from the service I told mother I had something different about my right hand and it would not close like the other. It was then that I learned what happened after I took the stove poker out of the window. The window pane had fallen across my hand and everyone thought my hand was cut in two. That was news to me and I now know why my hand was different.

William Henry (Bill) Heriford was born in Maysville on June 8, 1927.

The first year of school for J.R. took place in Berlin, Missouri at the consolidated school a few miles east of Berlin. It may have been the first consolidated school in Missouri. The school bus (and you must believe this) was a covered wagon and in winter was heated by an oil heater in the middle. We often traveled in snow so deep that the horses would balk and have to be whipped to get moving. Mean? No a necessary step since fifteen to twenty cold children had to get to school, rain snow or storm. I will never forget Mrs. Reasel Isaacson my teacher. I will also remember the little girl that needed a gallon tin can to complete her project for class. There seemed to be plenty of them on the farm where we lived so I took her one and received my first kiss from a girl.

It seems now that we had bigger snows then as the road from our house to the little town had either been cut to form a deep area for about two hundred feet or it had been washed out so many times that it turned out that way. During our first winter there the snow drifted in that area so deep that it was impassable for some time. The postman had to drive his horse and buggy through the farm to get around it and had to cut fences to make it to town.

Berlin was an interesting little town with lots of excitement going on. Halloween brought many mysterious happenings, like the time Bro. Billie's car was found on the awning over the front of the Hardwick store. And the day our old cow somehow climbed up on that roof. No one admitted to doing that but the Bowman brothers were considered the prime suspects since they owned the only steam tractor large enough to do such a thing. There may be only two witnesses to this alive today but you better believe it.

We lived on the next hill across from the church and one night a fire at the church lit up the whole countryside. This happen the day after I had gone to sleep in the pew and the family went home without me. Dad did come after me when they realized I was not with them. By the way, one of those Bowman boys became the pastor of President Harry Truman's church.

My first solo driving experience came at Berlin while I was in the first grade. Dad had an old touring car that I think was a Hupmobile and I was setting in it to play when something I pulled should not have been pulled. The result was a free ride down the driveway that ended when the car rolled into the garage and stopped, to some that was scary but I thought it was OK.

We lived in a farm-house a half mile from town that was surrounded by trees that were large and tall. During a heavy storm we were preparing to go to the cellar that had a smoke house over it when the wind got very strong. As we started out the back door one of those trees fell across the smoke house and crushed it. By the time the storm was over most of those trees were down and lying parallel along the north side of the house. We would have survived if we had gotten into the cellar but probably have waited a long time to be rescued from it. The next winter was very cold and houses were not insulated much then and we heated by wood stoves. One cold morning Dad got up and started the fire in the living room stove and we gathered around to warm up. We usually slept with the windows open for fresh air then whether summer or winter. When breakfast was ready we gathered in the kitchen to eat and someone smelled smoke. It was not from the cooking but from the wallpaper on the wall behind the living room stove. Dad put it out with a bucket of water but it made a mess of the wall and ceiling. That same winter the rabbits were looking for food around the well just outside the kitchen door and Dad thought that was for the next meal. He picked up the old 10 gage shot gun and slowly opened the door and bumped the door handle with, of all things, the trigger of the gun. The result was a loud blast that startled everyone and left a large hole in the ceiling and roof that we could see the moon through. A 10 gage makes a large hole.

Isaac Edward Heriford was born in Berlin on May 8th 1931.

King City was another place that doesn't bring many memories but some were exciting. Such as the time an uncle suggested I aim my toy gun at the light bulb. It wasn't as 'toy' as he thought and the bulb exploded and gave him a shock. It didn't really matter because we could not afford the electricity anyway. It still was bad for the uncle and I. My first major injury came while we lived there when visiting friends. I had tried to climb a small tree by standing on a wash tub that was upside down. The small limb I used to climb up was very week and broke leaving me head down on the edge of the tub. The result was a large gash just above my eye brow that bled like a major artery and covered my face with blood. With all the yelling that went on my mother came rushing out and put her dainty handkerchief on my head which immediately became red. A young man there had a convertible handy and drove me to a doctor in town where I watched while he sewed the large gash and said it will be good as new. I still have a very sensitive spot there that I had to protect for a long time.

Dad held revivals in several towns during his ministry and Whitesville was one I remember well. A boy I had befriended there attempted to slide down a rope in the barn but his grip was not enough to hold him and he slide all the way down. The result was a very serious burn that caused his fingers to grow together before they got him to the doctor in St. Joseph.

Joyce Elisabeth Heriford was born in King City on April 28, 1933.

Union Star was a place of many memories for our family. The drug store in town where the manager thought the Heriford kids needed milk shakes but couldn't afford it so he managed to give us one if we stopped for anything. The saddest thing that took place there was the death of a student that had climbed onto the transformer next to the schoolyard and was electrocuted. That same year a student that was a little rough at times took over the small swing and as he was swinging, drug his toe on the ground and broke it. He developed infection and died in less than two weeks from blood poison. There was a brighter side to life there. A family lived up the street from us by the name of Cederland?. They had a Saint Bernard dog that was a lot of fun and loved to pull us around on sleds or homemade skis. We made many friends in Union Star and most of them were from the Baptist church. I still remember many of the faces though not many names. The Laffoon family was one I will never forget. Hubert, the father, was Sunday school director and deacon and he and his wife had three sons and one daughter. The oldest son Lewis was my best friend and we spent a lot of time together. I, and sometimes my brothers, would spend the night with them on the farm. It was great fun to be able to run all over the farm to see what all we could discover. We picked berries of all kinds there including gooseberries. Snakes would often surprise us under the gooseberry bushes.

The river ran across their farm and we fished there often. Bobbie and Billy were the other two boys. They were younger but always wanted to be with the rest of us. I was surprised many years later to learn that Bobbie had gone to Tanzania as a medical missionary. His son is now a missionary in Malawi. One of those times that we spent the night with them will be remembered for a long time. In those days fresh air was considered a necessary part of life and we often left the windows open at night to have the fresh air, even in winter. This particular night four little boys crawled in one bed and pulled up the covers, with the windows open of course and arose to find several inches of snow on top of the covers. The cold didn't seem to mean anything to us and we had to play in the snow in our pajamas before trying to throw it out the window. Then we felt the cold and hustled to the kitchen stove to dress and warm up. Life was more fun then than it is in our old age. I shudder to think of that now but it was fun then.

I remember the churchyard with tables attached to the row of trees all ready to set up the Sunday afternoon dinners. That was real fellowship time and was a big part of the success of reaching out to the neighbors. It was also a time when the preacher's kids could act up at church. I can't recall much about the success of the ministry there but I'm sure many people remembered Billie Heriford for many years after we left there and even for generations. That was not because Billie Heriford was so great but because his life was dedicated to ministering to people of all races, positions in life and personalities. It was not him but the Holy Spirit that accomplished the work as Billie followed the Spirits leadership, not his own. I am convinced that if pastors were more considerate of what the Holy Spirit wanted than their own wishes churches would not be diminishing today.

We had many hucksters in those days that brought around fresh fruit and vegetables and sometimes fish. On one occasion one of them had big juicy grapefruit and they were good looking. Martha was so tempted she convinced Dad to let her buy one, one taste and she said it was a bad one because it was too sour to eat.

There was another family in Union Star that we knew quite well and I think my sister had a crush on the oldest boy. I don't remember his name but the family name was Files. Mr. Files had a printing shop there and he printed the county newsletter and probably other things as well, but I went with his son and visited the shop and found it interesting. He printed the paper on a 12x18 hand fed press. Another interesting thing occurred years later when my father and I went to the army air corps enlistment center to see if I could enlist. A tall handsome fellow came to wait on us and announced that he was Willis Cederland. He was the boy that had the Saint Bernard dog in Union Star.

The house where we lived in Union Star was on a farm and an orchard was very nice for playing. One hot summer the weather was very unpredictable and miserable. Dad moved the beds to the orchard one evening so we could sleep out in the little breeze. I was playing with my little sister and her arm hit the metal railing at the end and her arm was broken. Later as we enjoyed the night the weather changed and a storm blew in what turned out to contain a tornado. We rushed into the house and finished the night without beds. It took awhile to dry out the mattress and bedding. At another time we went to the cellar as a storm came up and when it had passed there was six inches of hail covering the ground. We also had a nice garden and could hardly wait for the potatoes to have little potatoes so we dig up some to eat. The whole family worked in the garden, with joy usually, since it would be our livelihood for several months.

We had an old barn on the lot that was not in use but had hay left in the loft. It was fun to climb up on the hay and slide down. One of those slides I missed the floor and fell ten feet to the floor of the barn. I was sure I had broken my back and I lay across an overstuffed chair for several days before I could stand to be touched. I had a small dog while we lived there and he began to chase the chickens. Dad grabbed a small board and chased him down and swatted him on the head, what he hadn't noticed was a nail in the end of the board and that was the end of my dog.

A fellow by the name of Wright operated a service station on the edge of town that I never knew very well but he had a brother that was crippled by polio and lived on the family farm. One week end he came into town on a trotter pony cart but it was not pulled by a pony. He had trained a pig very well and that pig was now big enough to pull him and the cart around. He made a big impression on the whole town.

Janice Heriford was born in Union Star on October 21, 1935.

From Union Star we moved to Clarksdale, Missouri a small town but a nice town. An uncle and his family lived there and he had a blacksmith shop. It was an interesting place to visit. There were machines, tools and gadgets everywhere and an occasional dog. The dogs were not a necessity but found it easy to crawl under the door to get in out of the weather. One such time a female expecting a litter found her way in and found one of the projects a nice place to hide. When they came in to work the new mother objected and would not let them touch the machine they needed to work on. They allowed her a few days to get the litter on their feet but had to resort to meanness to get her out. I won't tell that part of the story or OPCA might dig them up to investigate. The co-worker at that time was a preacher in training. Uncle David was a good mechanic and did everything including bodywork and repair. During the Second World War he was contracted to teach aircraft engine repair to army personnel. He later became involved in bodywork for insurance companies after the war ended. He was also quite humorous and enjoyed a practical joke now and then or when ever the opportunity arose. He had a jack hammer for shaping things in metal and enjoyed borrowing some ones watch and placing it under the hammer and tripping it. The result was a loud bang but he had set the hammer so it would not reach the watch. A look of fright and maybe anger appeared anyway.

I attended fifth and sixth grade in Clarksdale but most of it was held in an abandoned garage. The first year we were there the school burned down and the auto dealership left so school was held in their building. I was one of two in the fifth and sixth grade, both boys. Several classes met in one room with one teacher. There was a nice park in the center of town and we often played ball there for physical education. At one ball game I was batting and surprisingly hit the ball right back at the pitcher and it hit him between the eyes. That was the first time I ever saw anyone knocked out. He wasn't very happy with me.

A family lived a few miles east of town on a farm that had a beautiful spring they had built a small roof over and it made a nice place to set and watch the birds and animals as they came to drink. Cranes, herons, ducks and small animals enjoyed the nice cool water. We were often invited there to set and dine by the spring.

A small pond was in a field near where we lived and some of us went to wade in it on a warm day. The next day we notice cattle wading in it and feces floated in it. It was no longer inviting.

An elderly gentleman came into town with his produce loaded on his wagon to sell what he could. Usually by the time he had sold a few dollars worth he went to the drug store and got liquor to drink. After that everyone helped themselves to what was left. I think that was what he wanted.

We lived just across the road from the railroad and were often hosts to "bums" that needed food. Mother would tell them to set down on the porch and she would fix them a meal. Most of them were very polite and always thankful and we liked to hear them tell their stories. Mother never seemed to worry about them. A favorite Uncle of mine lived there for many years and his wife still lives there and hosts the family reunion every year. We moved to a small farm across town so we could have pasture for our cow and raise a pig. I guess we were fortunate to escape serious illness because we drank the milk straight the cow. I often wonder if pasteurizing ruins the milk. It tasted better then anyway. There were several pear trees on it and we picked a lot of pears and mother canned them. We also had a garden and raised vegetables for eating and canning. One summer a nearby farmer burned off his pasture and the fire extended to our garden. It was shocking to see the sweet corn on the stalks already popped. The chickens that often fed in the garden were quickly run from the garden by the fire.

Being a poor family we didn't take many vacations except to visit family but on a few occasions the whole family joined dad as he traveled out of state for revivals. One such trip was to Chickasha, Oklahoma where mothers' sister and family lived. We stayed with them in their small home and enjoyed their hospitality as well as to venture over the farm. I joined dad and Uncle Charles on a jack rabbit hunt and walked down to his watermelon field.

As we left a service at the small country church one night we encountered a truck that had trouble. The engine had stalled and he had no bakes and it had rolled back into the ditch. This would not have been too unusual except the truck was loaded with watermelon to the top of the cattle bed. As you might guess the melons destroyed the racks and spread down the ditch in a mess. We had gone there in a grain wagon with benches in it and Uncle Charles unhitched the horses and proceeded to pull him to the top of he hill at which point he instructed us to take all we wanted. We went there in a wagon designed to hall grain and it soon was so full we had to sit on watermelons all the way home.

Our cousin had a boy friend with her and they and Martha sat up late eating watermelon. I don't think they were alone because the next morning the wagon was empty.

Phase II
The Move to the Big City

In 1936 Dad was called to the Oakland Park Baptist Church in Kansas City, Kansas. A lot changed for us as we were not used to such a big city or school. We lived close to the church and could walk to church but we did have a car. I believe it was an Essex Teriplane. That would be a prize to own now for it was a beautiful car and would seat the whole Heriford family, which had grown to four girls and three boys.

The Nine Herifords

Joyce, Martha, Audra, Billie(William James) Mary, Janice, back row, Isaac, Bill J. R.

The school I was to attend was about two miles away and was a large school, Central Junior High. I was accustomed to one room in school and here I had to go to six different rooms before the day was over. I didn't like it to say the least and didn't do very well at first but when the new wore off and I felt more comfortable with more teachers I got by. My homeroom was the mechanics class although I was not enrolled in the class. My mathematics class was my favorite and I could keep up with the work as a breeze. The instructor, Mr.Kuckuk was nice and he gave a lesson in solving problems that I hope

15

stuck with others as well. He started the class by saying the answer to solving any problem was in knowing the principal or purpose. If you know what an object is supposed to accomplish the answer becomes simple. I believe that has helped me in many ways.

My English teacher was not as nice in a way but I guess I liked her anyway. I was supposed to give an essay and on the day I was to give it she called on someone else. Thinking I might not have to give it I didn't bring my written copy to school the next day. In fact I don't know what I did with it. She threatened to fail me and I didn't like that so I refused to give it.

She continued to threaten and I continued to be stubborn until the end of the year. When I got my report card I was a little surprised to have a perfect score for the year. I enjoyed English and still do but I didn't like her threats. One other thing I remember about Ms. English will always haunt me. She hated 'dangling participles'. To this day I shudder when I hear a preacher use 'dangling participles'. The first winter there the snow came very heavy and sleigh riding was great. Kansas City, Kansas had some long steep hills and many were closed because of the danger but sleds took advantage of that. One boy in my homeroom was a little too sure of himself and went down a hill that was not protected only to slide under a car going down the other street and was killed instantly. Sleigh riding was not as thrilling after that.

I entered Wyandotte High School in 1940, I think, and enjoyed all my classes there. Math, algebra, English and glee club were a breeze and I enjoyed them all but my favorite class was printing. The first two years consisted of learning the type cases and making up flyers and letters. The second year was spent learning the presses, which seemed to be my thing and along with setting type I was running the presses. The last year I and one other boy seemed to be the only ones interested in hand feeding the big cylinder press on which we ran the school paper and the school board monthly news letter. That other boy happened to be the son of the man I was later to work for at Missouri Baptist Press. I was often called from other classes to finish running the school paper. It had to go out you know. My final grade card there had perfect grades all through. I was not a genius; I just enjoyed what I was doing. That will make a difference in any ones life. I have a cup now that has the words "loving what you do is success' "doing what you love is success". Many things happened during those years in KC and I will never remember all of them. The bike ride I didn't deserve, on a borrowed bike with a front fender about ready to fall off. It didn't fall off it just stuck in the front tire and stopped it and sent me over the handlebars to the rough concrete. I still have scars on my elbows and knees from it and my belt was cut in two as I slid down the hill on my own.

I never was interested in girls until I entered the army but one girl wanted to change that. She was a nice looking flirt with long black hair. She seemed to think I liked her and her mother was no help at protecting me. I will well remember Marquita Timmerman but I don't know what happened to her. When we moved to the end of Fifteenth Street we had several kids to play with. The Huntington family had several kids and across the street from them lived the Shultz family with three. Behind them lived the Huganine family with two boys. One was diabetic and didn't play with us much. It was during this time I decided I needed a bike like the others but had no money to buy one. James Huganine had been hauling garbage and junk for people and I helped him pull his cart around to gather it and haul it to his back yard. He was filling a low spot and feeding rats. Environ-mentalists had not been awakened yet. As we gathered junk I found bike parts and began to salvage them so I could assemble my own bike. In less than a year I had my own bike and I decorated it with lights in the wheels and working brake lights. I soon became the bike decorator of the neighborhood.

I had gotten used to the change of environment but the country was still interesting. During summers I spent some time at my Aunt Martha and Uncle Omar Hammonds near Princeton helping with harvesting of grain and thrashing and baling hay. I enjoyed some time with cousins Lorene and Lawrence. It was always during the hot of the year but I could take it a lot easier then than when I grew old. We usually went to town on Saturday to shop and chat with the farmers from all around Princeton. I think they exchanged ideas as well as jokes but we boys just wandered around town. Our favorite hamburger was available for 5 cents then.

There were times when work was caught up and we gathered at Aunt Morge and Uncle Howard Casteels for home made ice cream and maybe cake. That ice cream was the coldest I ever tasted. It made my headache when I ate a little to fast but it was good. Uncle Howard raised livestock and Aunt Morge raised turkeys and chickens. She sold eggs as well as made cheese and butter to sell. I must tell about a boy that was also a distant relative. Jeanie Sims was very large and most people thought he was mute because he never talked. The men at harvest especially teased him and I think he liked it but he would never talk to them. He talked with Lawrence and I without any hesitation but not many others. He was considered lazy because he usually stood and watched. On one occasion Lawrence and I were to take a three-ton truck loaded with oats to the barn and unload it. It was necessary to shovel the oats into the grain room and took quite a while to do it. I told Lawrence I thought Jeanie was big enough to unload it by himself and Jeanie took the shovel and pushed us out of the way and unloaded the complete load faster than we expected to do it. When we told the rest of the men what he had done they laughed till they cried.

When we first arrived in Kansas City and Oakland Park Baptist Church the attendance there was probably about 40 or 50 per Sunday. Because of the love and compassion of my Mother and Father and the power of God the church grew rapidly and began to reach out to other neighborhoods. Soon after we arrived there I made my public profession to follow Christ. By the time I was 18 I had taught classes of young boys and learned that not every boy was as meek as I. It was a great experience for me and I am sure it was a part of my preparation for the future.

Our family was always a close one and we tried to work together at every task. On one occasion we had spent some time trying to decide where the rake had gone and who had used it last. It was found but not everyone knew it I guess. Several hours later Mary was wandering around the house from room to room and Dad asked what she was doing and her reply "I'm trying to find the rake". In the house? Dad asked. I could tell of many such funny happenings but I could never remember all of them.

I went to high school at Wyandotte High school in Kansas City, Kansas from 1940 to 1943. I enjoyed school and did very little home work as all my classes seemed so easy. I had a math and algebra teacher that was American Indian and very funny in several ways. Her name was Mrs. Shimalfinick. Often when she was disturbed or irritated by a student she would back up to the chalk board and bump her elbow against the chalk board. That usually made it hard for other class members to avoid laughter but they didn't dare laugh out loud. I seldom did any home work and on one occasion she called on me to put a problem on the board and work it for all to see.

Algebra was always easy for me but when I went to the front to fulfill her wishes she asked where my homework papers were. When I said I didn't have any she began her little display. I went on with the problem and without difficulty put the problem on the board. I was told I would flunk her class if I didn't do homework but at the end of the year she gave me a perfect score.

I took glee club my last two years and enjoyed singing which I still do. And participated in the schools operetta the second year. I also took printing class but was often called to help run the school paper when it was late getting started and would miss glee club. I participated in gymnastics and track but I never appreciated football or basketball. I still don't like to watch those sports on TV.

Phase III
In the service

Near the end of my last year at Wyandotte High I enlisted in the US Army Air Corps. The Air Force had not been formed as yet. I was accepted and went to St. Louis to a building where we went through some tests and sent back home to finish school. The tests we were to take included Math, English, History and etc. and took about four hours to complete. Along with that a test of our agility and response to see what we might be able to do. That part was fun for it was like an arcade and fun. July 21 I began my training in basic military in Miami Beach, Florida and so began a new way of life for me. As a small boy I saved Wheaties box tops and sent them in to get a small booklet about how to fly. I had no idea that I would ever be able to fly.

I was anxious to learn to fly but that was to take time. It was necessary to have some college training before learning to fly and a long stretch of orientation by the flight trainers. I did get to go on an orientation flight while in college at MM&M College in Houghton, Michigan but it was a brief flight in a piper cub. I was a bit puzzled when the pilot handed me a paper sack and said "you may need this". You can guess what it was for. Four months were spent in Michigan and the next step was Santa Anna, California. When we left Miami Beach for Houghton, Michigan we were dressed in our summer uniforms and arrived in Houghton to cold and snow and no coats. They were all in our luggage, which had not arrived yet. When we left there we were dressed in winter uniforms and arrived in sunny California where the temperature was 80 degrees. That trip out west had another special occasion. We had to change railroads in Kansas City and were able to meet family for a few minutes at which time I got my second kiss from a girl. More about that later.

Flight training involved more study than training. Meteorology, theory of flight, navigation and drilling were essential and that involved many hours. Morris code was an essential and we spent many hours trying to master it. Most of the time was in total darkness so we would not be disturbed by outside interest. That made it hard to stay awake while listening to a faint 'dah-dit-dit' for an hour. Aircraft identification was another requirement and that was learned by watching slides projected on a screen. I don't know how many planes we had to be able to identify but it was a lot. Aircraft from every nation had to be identified since we might meet any of them while in action. This also was done in darkness and put many to sleep but we had to take a test before completing the course. On one occasion a master sergeant was operating the projector and slipped in a slide that was not an aircraft. Out of fifty classmates I was the only one to identify that slide. It was a blond leaning over a table with large bossoms about to fall out.

Discipline was important to be sure but it seemed overly so in the cadet program. We had to stand square, sit square, eat square and sleep square. Only those who went through such a program would understand what that meant but it was true. When we entered the mess hall and approached the table we looked liked robots as we tried to step over the bench to be seated. As we ate the fork or spoon had to rise perfectly straight up till it was level with the mouth then straight to the mouth. That only lasted for a few weeks till the commander thought we had the idea.

Santa Anna was a large base and had numerous residents but I wouldn't guess how many. I only know parade drill practice covered a large field and involved many men. Other studies included nomenclature of all the weapons and equipment we might use in action. We had to dismantle and restore every kind of weapon available even though we might never use them. Since I have a big interest in machines and etc., I enjoyed that a lot.

We did no flying there but we saw a lot of planes flying from the marine and navy bases near by. The Marines flew P38 fighters and the Navy flew corsairs, both of which were very advanced high-speed fighter planes. It was interesting to watch them 'dog-fighting' at high altitude as though they were in the war zone. A problem developed in the P38s that was tragic and we were observers of the results. For some reason the P38s seemed to lose control at very high speed and several of them flew straight into the ground near our base, one within half a mile of us, and it was completely buried in the ground when it hit. Some pilots were able to bail out but the construction of the tail section made that dangerous as well.

The next step in my flying experience took place in Santa Maria, California. It was a commercial flight school contracted by the air corps to train pilots and most instructors were civilian. There were several army officers stationed there, to check on our training and to test us, and our abilities. This was an exciting step for me as we were to fly Steerman biplanes and those you could do anything with. Loops, slow rolls, snap rolls, fly upside down and any other aerobatics you could attempt. I soloed in the minimal hours and enjoyed an instructor that liked to try anything and encouraged me to do so. After a few lessons in aerobatics I tried different things and one was to do figure eights and include a snap roll at the top of each climb. A lazy eight involved going into a slight dive then pulling up into a steep climb till the plane was about to stall and then going into a steep turn to descend again. A snaproll was accomplished by pulling back on the stick to put the plane in a stall position and kicking the rudder either way to cause the plane to spin until it was back in the original attitude and reversing the controls. So I would go into a lazyeight and add a snap roll at the top with the turn. I did it the next time I was up with that instructor and he enjoyed the change.   That, without a doubt, was the most enjoyable time of my flying career. Accidents were rare there but one took place after we had been in training for several weeks and one young cadet that had high hopes but was misled. His father was a pilot in the army and he felt that made him a pilot. He didn't solo until the major insisted his instructor insist he take his solo flight. He made several attempts to land and finally landed crossways of the runway and almost hit the control tower. His landing was not successful and his flying career ended as well as his life. That was unnerving to say the least. That made us more aware of the need for discipline. When a pilot begins his flight he must check the plane over closely to be sure it is flight worthy. That is not an option. A personal ability check is a good idea too. I am not sure of the number of hours I flew there but every one was a joy. The joy of being up in Gods air and looking down at all He had created.

I think sheep were the main crop there as we had lamb chops, lamb roast or leg of lamb many times and I gained 20 pounds in the four months I was there.

The next step for my training was at Taft, California. The planes we flew there were low wing planes. They were Vultee Valiants or as we called them Vultee vibrators. That was because the Dual pitch props made a lot of noise and vibrations until you switched them to high pitch. Those were interesting to fly but were the beginning of navigational training for us. We didn't actually fly on instruments but learned the basics of instrument flight and instruments themselves. Our studies in flight school included navigation and how to plot a course but we were not involved in traveling as yet. Taft was a rather small town and we didn't spend much time in town but I remember a restaurant that served family style any kind of food you wish, American, Italian, Oriental, Mexican or a mix. We overate every time we went there.

Luke Field in Phoenix, Arizona was my next assignment for flight training. It was a large base a little west of town and we trained in AT 6s, a low wing plane with more power than we had experienced before. It was capable of doing some aerobatics but not as safely as the Steerman biplane. We were introduced to new things there that were important to flying fighter planes or bombers. Navigation became more important and required many hours of study. We had to plot a cross-country course and then fly it. If we goofed we were in trouble. Some did miss their mark but not tragically. On one case we were to fly at high altitude and get acquainted with using oxygen. We were to fly at twenty one thousand feet and report at three different airports as we flew over. The world looks different at that height and at night it was beautiful. When I looked down I could see the lights of homes and towns that looked almost like the stars overhead.

We were required to learn to fly with instruments only. After our instructor agreed that we were ready we had to fly with an observer in the front seat to watch for other planes or even the mountains that were all around Phoenix. I had very little trouble with that but some had a bit of claustrophobia being under the hood where you couldn't see out. My final test to qualify for instrument rating became one for history.

My check pilot was a major and gave me instruction to bracket the radio range close by and end up over a certain landing strip about 50 miles away. That strip was in the center of a range of mountains, and I was to fly to the strip and shake the 'stick' to let him know I thought I had arrived. I had carefully checked my watch at the right time so I was confident I was at the right point. The response I got after shaking the stick was nil. Realizing I was near mountains I shook even harder and still no response.

Then I knew something was wrong and didn't choose to take a chance so I removed the hood to be surprised to see no observer in the front seat. I then began to rock the plane sideways up and down and etc. only to see the major bounce up and down with the motion of the plane. I realized he had a problem and I turned to return to the field. To do so I should radio the field and notify them I had a problem but a new thing occurred to me, I couldn't because the control to the radio was in the front seat and I was on the wrong frequency. Well so much for notifying the tower, I'd just have to fly in any way. As I approached the field another surprise appeared. The landing gear hydraulics control was in the front seat. I could not lower the landing gear.

The time had come for me to remember the procedures we were to follow. It would be necessary to buzz by the tower to let them know I had a problem and fly out again and wait for instructions. Of course with no radio I couldn't get instructions so I decided I would fly by, go out of the pattern and watch for the fire trucks and emergency vehicles to appear and then return to see what would happen next. As I flew by the tower and gave it full throttle to go around the major rose up and said "OK I have it". I think my blood boiled a little about that time but I let him land it. After we landed and he was grading my paper he asked if I had accomplished the task and said he had been to a party that night and had very little sleep. I should have told my regular instructor or reported him, for that put two pilots in grave danger. We could have collided with another plane or a mountain and that story would never have been told. I hope he never forgot that experience.

During this training a Link Trainer became a big part of our life. It had everything just like the cockpit of a plane and was mounted so it would swivel and turn, just like a plane. It would even stall out and go wild if you failed to maintain flying speed. We would get in it and close the door and be in total darkness until the instrument lights came on. An operator sat at a table outside and controlled a simulated plane that actually traveled around on a map as I 'flew' the planned course by instruments. It was a challenge but I enjoyed it and spent at least 50 hours in one, an hour at a time. This was for practice for instrument flight.

I enjoyed flying the AT6 and the formation flying was a thrill. We flew in groups of three and at times our props would almost touch the leaders' wing tips. We did loops, rolls and turns in that formation and it was a thrill to be sure. Discipline again was important.

As we progressed in training we had to practice low flight as though we were on a bombing run. During one of those runs an instructor and student, one of twins at the base, flew too low and clipped one of those famous Arizona cacti and crashed the plane. We flew those runs at about 250 miles per hour and you can imagine what that plane and occupants looked like. It was sad because the twin brother had to travel home with the body of his brother.

I have been amazed at the changes that have taken place in Phoenix since then as we often would go into town and run clear across town and back in fifteen minutes. Now I doubt if I could even find that part of town. I had several friends in the service and one was an Arabic young man by the name of Shirally Karim. We played pool together often on the base as well as in town and were good enough that most players would leave the pool hall as soon as we walked in. He was a good fellow and I have wondered about him often since I left the service. Another good friend was Lewis Jamison from California. He had a habit that I wouldn't want but he seemed to survive. He liked to gamble and put his heart in it. Or maybe I should say his pocketbook. At one time he had a 1936 Auborn automobile that every one on the base would love to own and he bet it in a poker game and lost it. It didn't matter to him much because the tires were worn thin and we couldn't buy tires then. It wasn't long till he won back his cab company in Long Beach so he was happy. Several years later he was in Kansas City and called me at work and told me to come to the airport and go for a ride in his commuter plane. He was running a flight service and had brought someone to KC and decided to find me. Georgia and I went right away and flew around over KC in his Stinson Reliant.

I could never remember all the fellows I knew but others included Larry that got married in the service and his wife went with me to church at some bases. He was Catholic and she a Baptist. Then there was John Hughes. He was a fun guy and the life of the party, sometimes to the chagrin to all of us. We visited LA one weekend and there was no hotel to go to so we decided to go to the all night theatre and watch cartoons. Following the cartoons a movie was shown I believe it was "Salome How She Danced" and at the first romantic scene John broke into a laugh like a mad man and we were instantly ejected. Some 'night on the street' that ended up at the bus stop until the next morning.

Then there was Jankowski, with all the black hairs on his chest that sat around the barracks with a lighter and lit the hairs on his chest just to stink up the place. He also had a problem with drinking but stuck to cheap wine so he could get more for his money. That stuff seemed to revive every time he got a drink of water and on one occasion at the wrong time. On a Sunday morning we were to take a long flight and we had tried to keep him away from the water fountain, but just before we went to the plane he found one and by the time we reached the plane he was drunk. That was a no-no and the end of his flight training.

Each time we graduated from a step in our training, the officers planned a party for us as though they were very glad to see us leave. The final one was at Luke Field and it was a big one. We were all in our new officer uniforms and feeling spiffy so the USO invited lots of young girls to dance with us and help us party. I was never a dancer or drinker so I sat on the side most of the time. One girl that was in college there came and insisted on teaching me to dance. By the time I had stepped on her second toe she agreed I was not a dancer. That same evening we were to ship out and head for home for two weeks and since there was no place to stay to wait for the 4 o'clock train she insisted I go to her house and her mother would wake me early to catch the train. Since I had no other plans I agreed and we had a nice visit and went to bed. The next morning her father roused me and drove me to the station. Her mother had to go along for some reason and as they left me she told me her daughter was surprised that I never made a pass at her.

I fully enjoyed my time in the service because our family had always taught discipline at home and the army taught me more about the need for discipline. Many interesting things took place during those two years and besides loving to fly, the activities in schooling as well as in the barracks were interesting. We lived in large barracks with bunk beds in a long row and without privacy. The latrine was also without privacy and consisted of a long row of showers, a long row of urinals and a long row of stools. There seemed to be a tendency to flip a towel at an unsuspecting bare bottom and that often started a slight row. With the stools all in the open occasion often arose to enjoy the shock of another fellow cadet, by either reaching over and flushing his stool while he was deep in concentration or laying a smoldering cigarette butt on the stool as he started to sit down. That often started more than a small row. When we were in the barracks we were always alert to an officer entering as it was required that we stand at attention when one enter the room. The first to see an officer approach was to yell 'attentut' at which time we stopped what ever we were doing, whether dressed or undressed, and pop to attention at the end of the bunk. One buddy was just getting into his pants when some one yelled 'attentut' and he fell across the floor and finally drug himself to the end of his bunk and stood with his pants around his ankles. On another occasion someone yelled 'attentut' and every one 'pop to' but no officer came in. That was a 'no-no' and the responsible person was attacked by the whole barracks.

I must back up and tell of our upbringing. My father being a preacher and Mother a devoted preachers' wife made life very interesting for us. We knew the Bible was important and worthy of studying. Every evening was spent reading the bible stories and having prayer. It was the natural thing for us and everyone should have done the same thing because it has been the strength in our entire lives. I was anxious to be able to read it myself and found a very small dictionary to carry in my pocket. It didn't have all the bible names in it but taught me how to pronounce them. I carried that dictionary with me for many years and after my Mothers death it was found in her possession. I would like to have it for a keepsake now. As children we were well versed in the scripture and knew it's meaning for us and it will always be important to us. As we grew older we became more involved in the church and its ministry. Martha, Mary, Bill and I enjoyed singing and often went to Dad's revivals to sing as a quartet and some at other churches and events. I think most of us became involved in teaching pretty early.

Many things occurred during my time in the service and the most inspiring was the times I spent studying my Bible. The most popular thing to do on weekends was going to town to get drunk. That never appealed to me, and the day rooms where we could play pool or table tennis were always filled, so I took the opportunity to read. My Bible was the only book that seemed of interest and it became more so as I started from the beginning for a second time. Many times fellow soldiers would stop by and ask why I read the Bible. I usually told them I thought it was great history and we should all know the history that might be repeated some day. As time went by the questions began to turn into interest and they joined me with their Bibles. At times as many as fifteen were setting on the edge of their bunks reading and discussing the Bible and it's teaching. That inspired me to read it nine times while I was in the service so more would continue to join us. I have no idea how many were brought closer to the Lord by this but I continue to be hopeful. I tried to participate in the choir at each base because I enjoyed singing. The chapel at each base had Chaplains but not all had protestant Chaplains. In fact I was very disappointed at some of them because their daily lives did not meet my expectations.

Phase IV
Home again

I have mentioned my brothers and sisters earlier but I must go back and include their offspring since they will be involved in my future. Mary was the first of the family to marry and she and Ralph Farris had the first grandson in the Billie Heriford family. He was named James Everett b: 9-17-44 and became an embarrassment to his mother as they walked the streets of Hannibal, MO. At five years old he had learned too much, and as they walked down Main Street he saw this lovely girl across the street and gave a wolf whistle that would embarrass a teenager. Mary was shocked to say the least. They later had three girls to enter the picture who were given the names Pauline Faith b; 10-9-51 Kathleen Hope b; 9-21-55 and Aileen Grace b; 9-17-53. They were cute and smart and still are and each have their own families.

Martha married James Bell and they had two sons, Donald Earl b;1-1-47, Harold Dean b;9-30-50 and one daughter Patricia Ann b;4-6-48. Jim passed away and Martha remarried to Roy Marlow.

J.R. married Georgia Lee Shultz Heriford November 22, 1945 and they had two girls and three boys. Gladys Lorene, b; March 28, 1947. James R. Jr. b; August 4, 1949, Herbert

Leland, b; November 25, 1952 Mark William b; February 25, 1957, and Rosamond Bernice, b; April 25, 1961

William married Helen Ridge Heriford and they had four children. Robyn Elane b; 9-17-53, James Morgan b; 1-7-55, Megan Paige b; 4-27-63 and Laura Dilys b; 4-10-66.

Isaac married Patricia Ann Burrell Heriford and they had six children. Larry, b; March 11, 1952.D March, 1995. Jerry, b;May 14, 1954. Terry, b August 9, 1955. John, b; February 23, 1957. Crystal b; June 23, 1959. and Trina b; February 1, 1963. Isaac and Pat adopted Mark and Charles in the early eighties. Isaac married Tina August 20, 2002.

Joyce married J. R. Evans and they had two daughters. Audra Raylene b; 12-18-50 and Joyce Carlene b;4-17-52.

Janice married John Cambell and they had four children. William Joseph b; 7-17-1954, Pamela Janice b; 9-17-1956, Gary Wayne b; 2-1-1960 and David Lynn b; 7-6-1963.
She later married Arthur Hill and they had three children. Arti Jane b; 1-25-1966, Sharmon June b; 10-18, 1965 and Edward Arthur b; 1-15-1970.

At the completion of flight school we had to train in the planes we were to use on the frontline. However we did have two weeks to visit at home and I found a houseful waiting to welcome me home. Family, cousins, and that little girl from Pacific Street were all there.
        That was a very short visit and I had to travel to Yuma, Arizona to learn to fly B17 bombers. I had chosen to fly P51 fighters but that was not my lot. P51s were fairly new and were fast and very maneuverable and looked great. Instead of fighter planes I began training in the B17s and that included training

for gunners as well. We flew low past some large barrels so the gunners could practice shooting at them. There were also some P39s in a near by base and they were covered with heavier metal and the gunners practiced shooting at them as they flew by us. The guns they used were 50 caliber machine guns but had soft colored bullets that left a stain on the barrels or planes. Following four months of training there we were sent to Lincoln, Nebraska to be assigned to crews.

By that time the air force declared the B17s obsolete and we were unassigned for four months. Four months with nothing to do till they decided what to do with us. When we arrived we were assigned to barracks and told to check the bulletin board every day for the next assignment. No formations or class but just set around and wait. There was a chapel there but no chaplain so I went in town to the Methodist Church a few times. Lewis Jamison had gone home during the leave time and purchased a 1931 Model A ford and put a McCullah drone engine in it. It was very high compression and required petcocks installed so it could be started. It was much more powerful than the original engine and Lewis enjoyed that. On Easter Sunday a snow storm buried the country in twelve inches of snow but Lewis wanted to take me to church in his creation so off we went spinning and swirling down the highway. It was fun since no one else was on the road but when we got to town the churches were all locked up.

During that time I took time to run home to KC and visit with family and that little girl from across the street. I would go to the school and walk home with her. I even walked around the halls a few times and that officer's uniform got a lot of attention from others but I don't know if she was impressed. Finally new assignments came out and I was transferred to Blytheville, Arkansas and the troop carrier command and was to fly C46s to the east coast and pick up other crews and carry them to the west coast to prepare to ship to the pacific war zone. That didn't last long because the Japanese surrendered and the war was over. That announcement brought real excitement and the WACs came running out of the barracks screaming with joy. Some dressed only in their undies. That was an exciting day for all of us but since I didn't have sufficient months to qualify for discharge I didn't know what to expect. Soon after the war was officially over a bulletin was posted that any that wanted to leave should sign the roster. I enjoyed flying but I didn't plan on spending life in the service so I signed the roster. The very next day I received orders to travel to Leavenworth, Kansas to be mustered out. I had not expected that but it was OK and in two weeks I was out of the army.

Phase V
Back home

Returning home to stay sounded great and I didn't have to wait long to see what my future would hold. Dad had ordered some stationary printed in a little shop where I had worked a little before going away. I was sent there to pick them up and made the mistake of telling the owner that I had worked there for the former owner. I was hired and spent 13 years as a printer pressman and instructor of many young men. I have to take some time to tell of that experience. Charlie Couts and Tom Lance were the owners and operators and had built up a good business.

I had taken printing class at Wyandotte High School for three years and after returning from the service I began to work there and continued for thirteen years. Charles Couts and Tom Lantz were partners in the business and I was the first employee. My work included every part of the printing business. Typesetting with monotype, building forms, putting them in the chase and printing them was my main job. Other minor things would be inserted at times but operating the presses was my real joy. I like to make even an old machine run like new and this was great for me. Five presses were in use there and I operated any one of them and some times three or four at a time. Since they were automatic feeders I could start one, get the next one ready and start it running and while checking each one begin to prepare the next one. Tom and Charlie worried about what I was doing but since it meant money in their pocket they never complained. At that time as now I like to be busy and active. That not only relaxes your mind but makes a day go by faster. One project was laundry check tags for a laundromat. It required thousands of them so we printed them eight on a sheet and numbered them as we ran them. They were numbered on both sides which made the project more complicated because the numbers had to be the same on both sides and it was necessary to watch them close to make sure none was skipped. Also each sheet had to be turned over before running back through so the numbers would match. By attaching a small piece of chipboard on the delivery I was able to get it to flip the sheet over and thus avoiding the process of going through the pile of papers to turn them over.

The form was made up of thousands of tiny pieces and locked in a chase to set in the press. On one occasion the form had come loose while setting over the weekend and as the press was started the form flew all apart and the pieces fell under the press. It took several hours to reassemble the form before we could proceed. While running those on one occasion the feeder dropped one sheet and I tried to grab it to put it in it's order but the point at which I grabbed was at a point where the platen lock came to just one eighth of an inch. The result was my finger tips suddenly became one eighth of an inch thick, ouch.

I also had to operate the paper cutter and on one occasion as I cut and trimmed letterheads for some business Charlie bumped the cutter handle and the blade came down across the end of my index finger and almost severed the end of it. The paper cutter was a hand operated one with a long handle and this handle was almost vertical and easily knocked off balance. I grabbed a piece of wrapping tape and wrapped around my finger and continued working while Charlie sat in his chair in a daze or shock.

Charlie was a very rude and vulgar person with very foul language but he was also very weak in other ways. Tom was very calm and self controlled and seldom raised his voice. I guess they fit together pretty well.

Tom was a very quiet man and pretty reasonable but Charlie was very rude with his language. He was using the Lords name in vain and using very vulgar language. Even in the presence of Women. He had a very different out look on life. At one time as a youth he attended church and had gained a good knowledge of the Bible. The only problem was he developed a feeling of doubt after being challenged by an eager evangelist and decided he was an atheist. He really enjoyed arguing with anyone that would listen to him about the Bible and if they were not well versed in the Bible he would really make them feel foolish. I never challenged him because he seemed to see something different in me and never started anything with me. After I left there and moved to Hannibal, Mo. He became sick and tried to call me but I was not at home enough to take his call. I have wondered often of his demise. Tom, as I said, was a nice guy and worked hard to see that the company made a profit. One morning he went in early to get ahead a little and slipped as he was cutting paper and severed his hand at the wrist. When I came in Charlie was sitting at his desk in shock and had offered no help for Tom. I had to call the police to get an ambulance and the policeman took him to the hospital himself. Charlie could not go near the paper cutter for some time without getting faint.

We had five presses, all automatic feeders and I worked on any of them and sometimes two or three at a time. We were paid by the number of pieces we produced until the unions convinced the government everyone should be paid by the hour. A new law cut my wages severely.

Phase VI
The Question

During my employment at Couts and Lants I began helping a young lady by the name of Georgia with a newsletter for the youth of the association. We soon became more and more involved. I had not abandoned the little "lady from across the street" but had begun to realize we were not talking to each other but were just 'together'. We were just too timid to talk. The time I spent with Georgia seemed to grow and one day I invited her to go with me to visit a Spanish mission. I accused her mother of telling her to go but she said it was her own decision. After the meeting, which she did not enjoy because she could not understand Spanish, I asked the question that I think she was expecting. She said she would have to think about it but it didn't take her long to say OK. What does a young man do when he gets the answer he really expected but wasn't sure he wanted? Faint? Maybe wish he hadn't asked? I was ready for the answer and plans were soon begun for a wedding.

Our wedding was a quiet one compared to many but it worked for near 60 years. We were married on Thanksgiving just as the Thanksgiving service ended. We walked up the aisle and dad performed the ceremony as expected. We were driven to her parents, Arthur William and Bernice BeBelle Shultz for the dinner and soon left for Topeka Kansas for our honeymoon. That was a memorable trip since we went in the 1931 ford coupe I had just bought and put an exhaust heater on the night before. It wasn't completely finished and it would get too hot and I would have to cover the vent until it got cold and then uncover it again. It was snowing and cold that night but we made it to the Kansas Hotel and were glad to get out of the weather.

Combining ideas and interests is not a simple thing for two people of different gender. We were about to learn more about that. We had saved very little for the occasion and were now faced with deciding where to live. I previously mentioned the model A Ford I had bought just before the wedding so we had transportation. The 'where' was solved quickly by her mother, as she invited us to live in the little apartment above them. It wasn't elegant but neither were we so it became home for some time. The only problem was the fact that we had to go through their bedroom to get to the stairway to the apartment. Aunt Eunice lived in the basement apartment but she remarried and moved out so we took that until my father-in-law and I could build a basement next door on a lot I was able to buy for $150. That was a slow process as we did it all by hand and with hand tools. We dug the basement out with shovel and wheelbarrow. Poured the footing with hand mixed concrete and laid the foundation with 12 inch concrete blocks.

The fourth of July approached as we were laying the foundation and for several days we would find unexploded fire crackers laying in the foundation. One day Gramps picked one up and lit it and tossed it in the front yard. As with most cats, his own cat, sitting on his porch, saw the object land in the yard and ran over to investigate. When he saw it fizz he backed away a short distance and when it exploded he flew off to hide for three days under their porch.

I managed to get a loan to buy lumber to put a roof on the foundation and we lived in a basement house for three years before adding the upper part. That was almost ready for us to move in when our first little girl was born. Gladys was a sweet little baby and slept well in the day but seemed to prefer having colic at night. Her first few months were a little hectic but Pa slept well through it all. Mom was good at taking care of her most of the time. I don't know if Georgia was very happy with that little house but it was home and that she was ready for. We had everything needed to live and a good bed to sleep in. Our little kitchen may have been small but at least we had a stove, a refrigerator, a sink and dinning room set and that was sufficient for the time. That refrigerator caused Gladys to doubt her mothers' love one day when she was just learning to walk good. She walked into the kitchen to see what mom was doing and Georgia had the frig open to get something. Georgia leaned over to kiss her and get her to move so she could close the frig and we learned the frig was not grounded and they both got a shock. Gladys of course cried and wasn't sure she wanted her mother to pick her up. She seemed to forget it soon.

Having finished the basement enough to live in, my brother-in-law Bill Shultz and I decided we should take some time to fish so we built a boat out of sheet metal and I designed a propulsion system that I had thought about for a long time. It was fashioned after the tail of a fish and worked quiet well.

The only problem was the weight of the boat. It floated OK but was heavy to move in and out of the back of a pickup. That year was a rather unusual year for weather and the last week of December was like summer. So on New Years Day Bill and I decided to go fishing. We got up early and loaded into the Plymouth and headed for the lake. It didn't take long to get the rods set and it seemed a little cold so we went up to the car to wait for the fish to bite. The car was nice and warm from the trip there so I turned on the radio. The first sound we heard was "it turned cold last night and the temperature is now 1 degree". It didn't take long for us to get our fishing gear and head back home. Many things happened at that little house that made it interesting. I guess the most tragic was the occasion that forced me to get back to work on the house above. I had put a flat roof on the house hoping I would be able to finish it soon. Time went by too fast and the flat roof began to leak just a little bit now and then. Now and then ended in the middle of the night when we were all asleep and the celatex could not hold it any longer and came down with several gallons of water right in the middle of our bed. Georgia said enough was enough and if I didn't finish the house she would move back next door. I had help from brothers, brother-in-law, father-in-law and a few others in building the basement but the house was my own lot. I began working on it at 5 or 6 in the morning and went to work at 8 and returned to the house to work a few minutes and eat and head back to work till 5 and back to work on the house. I don't know just how Georgia felt about the progress but she helped at times when the two 'youngens' were alright.

Georgia also found herself working for the printing shop as work got heavy. We did a lot of forms for businesses and they had to be collated or assembled in sets and bound in some way. I would carry the paper home and she would do the collating and get paid 75 cents for every 1000 sheets of paper she handled. Doesn't sound like much but when you consider 50,000 sheets it adds up.

It took me three months to get the house where we could move in and a few more before it was finished but it was done. After we moved upstairs my sister Martha was in need of a place to stay so I let them move into the basement. A very small house for one family and now there were two families. I'm not sure how many children she had then but at least two and we had two. That made a crowd and crowds don't get along very good for very long. So I had put a fence around the front yard to keep Gladys and Dick off the street and now I had to put a fence between the front and the back to keep the kids separated. We all survived until the next event and that one was bad.

Before I go to the next step in our life I want to go back and reminisce and mention things about the family and what took place at the church that was very much a part of our lives. Dad was the pastor and the church was growing fast. It soon became necessary to consider enlarging the building. We were living on 13th street when we first moved there and the church was on 14th just a block south of us and 1 block west. For reasons that I am not aware of we moved to 15th street but it was still close to the church. While we lived there a family of Shultz's lived a few houses up the street and had a son Bill that was a little younger than I but we became close friends and played together a lot. I had made me a bike from discarded parts and we rode around town a lot together and even as far as Bonner Springs that was about 8 miles west. There was a railroad bridge on the way there that had a pretty nice swimming hole where the water had cut a deep hole at the bridge and we often went there to swim. On one occasion on a beautiful day in March we stopped to check it out and since it was 75 degrees the water looked great and clear. Without a care we stripped off and jumped in to find the water was about 40 degrees and we made a quick exit and back in our clothes and on to Bonner Springs. The Shultz's also had a daughter Georgia. I didn't pay her much attention then, or her me.

Across the street from the church was a vacant lot with a large embankment on the back of it. I'll go back to that later because it became a big part of this story. The church was on a narrow lot, probably 50 feet, and it set back from the property line only fifteen feet. The idea of expansion would necessitate getting permission to build almost to the curb. The building committee was able to get that permission and work was begun right away even though the money was not yet accumulated. The members were eager to see the building up and soon raised the money. That project almost doubled the size of the auditorium and that was soon filled. That new building was the sight of our wedding. Our family moved again this time a little farther away. The church was located on 14th street at Pacific Street and we moved to 11th street on Pacific Street. I remember many things that took place there but especially that Martha had begun to play the piano and we all liked to sing. Mother was an excellent pianist and Martha soon became one. We would gather around the piano and Mother or Martha would play and we would sing till the neighbors would come and join us. That house holds many memories such as the time we went off to church and no one thought to shut off the water heater. Not many were automatic then and we had to light it and shut it off when we were through. When we returned from church the heater had heated the water all the way to the neighbors' house and would have exploded soon if we had been later. That ruined the meter and a new one had to be installed soon. Bill was to wash dishes later and in an unhappy mood hit the faucet handle a little hard and the ceramic handle broke and pierced his palm to leave a bad cut.

I was given the task of killing the chicken for dinner and since I had been experimenting with electricity I decided to electrocute the chicken with my high voltage system. Instead of dying the chicken stretched out straight and squawked till every one inside the house could hear it. I wasn't praised for that. I had been playing with coils, transformers and radios and rigged a coil to the door handle of my room. I didn't like others coming into my room and messing with my old radios that I had restored. As you might guess Mother was the first one to enter. The shock didn't impress her and I had to remove it. Pronto. We lived here when I was called into service and the family moved again while I was away.

Back to the church. After our wedding the church grew rapidly and more space was needed. Not because of our families growth but because more people were coming. The lot across the street from the church was wide but because of the steep embankment on the back half of it, building there didn't look too good. Contractors were contacted and bids taken and a building fund was initiated to raise the funds. The rest of this story became a sad one as the contractor failed to reinforce the back wall of the basement enough and as the concrete was poured it bowed out till the concrete was two feet thick at the top. He knew he was losing money on it so he stopped work and the church had to get a lawyer and sue him and his bonding company to get it finished. That drug out for two years and it seemed impossible because we would have to raise more money to finish it. His bonding company did pay for the damage and the work was completed so we could meet in the basement, which we did for just a few years.

In the mean time Dad felt the need to move and was called to Hannibal, Mo. to pastor Calvary Baptist Church there. Georgia and I stayed there for some time until the rest of the building was completed. One bright Sunday we had driven the model A to church but Georgia thought it was too nice a day to ride and wanted to walk home. It wasn't far so I agreed but she wasn't happy about the next step. I got in the model A and started it and put it in low gear then got out and walked beside it steering through the window all the way home. Don't try that with an automatic or any car today. Several pastors served at Oakland Park after Dad left but things did not go well for some time. So many members thought every pastor should be just like Bro. Billie and that didn't happen.

We were members at Oakland Park Baptist Church for several years and I was elected a deacon when I was just twenty one and served for several years. I had taught Sunday School in a junior boys class from the time I was seventeen. Following my time in the service I returned to continue as a deacon and soon chosen as chairman. That became a difficult time as the pastor was not the best for the church. Differences arose as to what should be done about the pastor and it was obvious unity was absent. I was accused of being two-faced by a young lady that had been special to me and I was obviously hurt by her remarks. I had tried to be as neutral as possible but that was difficult because I felt the subject had been approached in the wrong way. The pastor finally resigned and soon after Georgia and I decide to attend a small church that was closer to where we lived.

Many misunderstandings arose and the church lost ground for a while. It did recover and is still alive. During that time the flood of 1951 hit and a lot of homes were destroyed in the Armordale, Rosedale and other low areas and houses were badly needed. We were approached, by a realtor, about selling our house to a veteran that had lost everything. I had heard about a small farm for sale and began to check into it. We were able to sign a temporary contract to buy it but it hinged on the sale of our house. It took several months for the veteran to get approvable to buy our house and secure a loan and the elder gentleman we were buying from passed away. It became necessary for the realtor to contact all heirs and get their signatures before the deal could go through. It finally was accomplished and a new era began in our life.

A family we had known for some time was one of those left without a home after the flood. He was Fritz Criswell but I don't remember his wife's name. They had a daughter and a son named Paul and one named Gerald. Soon after the flood they bought a farm west of town where we went hunting several times. Georgia accompanied me on one of those for her first hunting trip. While we were there Fritz gave me two guns that had gone through the flood. They were both unique so I kept them and still have the twenty two rifle that was made in 1914. After cleaning the barrel it turned out to be a good rifle and still is very accurate.

Phase VII
The Farm

That little farm was a 15 acre plot that was situated in the middle of a large plot and a half-mile dirt road for a driveway. It was winter when we moved there and getting colder every day. The house was not insulated and the doors and windows leaked air when the wind blew so we had to keep covers close for everyone. It had a coal furnace and only a small space for coal storage in the 'basement'. I had to hall coal in the car because the coal company would not deliver it up that road lest they get stuck. Most of the time I could not get to the house because the snow was so deep and had to carry the coal for half a mile or use the sled to haul it there. We survived that first winter but having to carry a baby boy (Herbie) all that way was as difficult as the coal when the snow was deep. The next spring looked better and I began to dig out more of the basement to make room for more coal as well as be able to install a pump in the well so we could have running water from the well. The well was on the back porch and that was not too difficult but the weather was not so cooperative. That spring became very wet and the wall of the foundation was not very sturdy. With the digging a long way from finished the wall collapsed into the basement and buried the conveyer I had designed to carry the dirt out. I had a small engine with a cable attached to a cart that was mounted on a special ramp so it would pull the cart up and dump the dirt as it reached the top of the ramp. I was not interested in giving up yet so I dug out enough to build a concrete block wall in its' place so I could continue the work on the basement.

By the time I had installed the water pump and piped the water to the kitchen the summer had arrived and the rainy season was in full swing. One afternoon on a beautiful day I noticed a very dark cloud to the west of us and it had formed a very straight line of black. I knew this meant wind and closed the doors and windows and gathered the family to the center of the house. That cloud approached rapidly and as I looked out the front door I saw a small elm tree bending to the south till it was lying almost flat but suddenly it was lying flat toward the north. The rain began to blow in under the door so I rushed everyone to the basement hoping the house would survive. The wind was very strong and we heard glass shatter upstairs but we stayed there till the wind calmed down. The house survived but about twenty peach and apricot trees were destroyed and my double garage was three feet to the north and three feet to the east. It also was not totally vertical any longer.

I had bought four calves to fatten that summer and after that storm everything dried up. The pasture became a desert and the pond dried up and the corn did no good. I lost money all around but it was an experience to remember. I sold the calves for the same amount I had paid for them and had hauled water and feed for them for the "never dried up before well" did dry up and we had to hall water from town.

After the storm a wire going to the garage had fallen and Dick playing with his wagon picked it up and was stuck to it when Mama heard him cry and thought he was dead but grabbed the wire and jerked it loose. He survived but Mama was very shook up. At another time there Herby in diapers had ventured out and a neighbor called to say a baby in diapers was walking down the street. He apparently was following his big sister to school.

A new friend arrived and I think the Lord sent him. A gentleman that was looking for property to build homes on came by and made us an offer that was too good to pass up and another odd thing took place. His neighbor, Paul wanted to buy his house when he bought other property. So we went to look at Paul's place and liked it very much and began negotiating. It turned out we were all dealing with the same loan agency and we just signed papers in the presence of an agency representative and the deal was closed. The agent couldn't see why he wasn't getting any money out of the deal. Our new home was on 43rd street in a nice neighborhood and on a 75'by 300' lot. The house set back from the curb about 75' and left a nice front yard for the kids to play in. It was also inviting for neighbor kids and that made everyone happy having friends to play with.

I did a little remodeling on this house so the girls and boys could have their own bedrooms. It had an attached garage and I put a floor in it and redid the garage door into a wall with a small window in it and built bunk beds on the wall for the boys. It made a nice room and they had room to play when the weather was bad.

Gladys will remember that place well because of one pet we had ordered from Spiegels catalog. With so much yard it sounded good to have something to enjoy the grass. So I ordered a Mexican burrow. When it arrived by train the man in charge of the shipments called me at work and said I have the symbol of the Democratic Party at the station and she is on a leash like a dog. By then I had bought a 1939 Pontiac four door and I had to put her in the back seat to get her home. It wasn't a problem because she was about the size of a large dog and I could pick her up and carry her easily. She became the pet of the neighborhood and enjoyed the big back yard where she had plenty of grass. It didn't take long for her to grow to a pretty good sized burrow and able to carry me around. They never trot or gallop like a horse but rather run in a nice smooth gait. Donnie Bell decided to ride her and with great gusto he yelled 'YAHOO' and the burro left without him.

The kids and nieces and nephews all enjoyed riding her and she was never bothered by them. In fact she seemed to enjoy the attention. As she grew in size she also grew in wisdom. She soon found out that she could lean against the fence and it would slowly give till she could walk over it. She also learned the secret to getting the gate open. It was on one of those occasions that she got out and was walking around in the front yard when Gladys decided to go get her back in the fence. I don't thing she was angry but just playful but as Gladys walked behind her a hind leg flew up and caught Gladys right in the eye. It didn't damage the eye but it put a big gash through her eyebrow and about thee inches above. It was bleeding profusely and a neighbor heard her cry and came over to help her only to find Momma sitting as if in a coma and faint. The shock of seeing Gladys so bloody was too much for her and it was a miracle the neighbor showed up to wrap a towel around her head and drive them to the hospital.

I was called at work and drove at about 90 miles per hour to get home only to find they were already at the hospital that was only a few blocks from where I worked. The doctors did a great job fixing her up and now at 59 the scar is hard to find. Imagine my daughter is almost 60, and that makes me feel old. We decided to sell the burrow because she had gotten too smart for that lot and fence but it was a sad time for all.

Before we sold the burrow we had a watermelon feast with Georgia's family present and a large washtub of rinds was left setting next to the fence where Jenny could reach over and eat the rinds. It was not my intention but she enjoyed the opportunity and truly gorged on melon rinds. The next morning she was rather listless and I noticed then that the rinds were all gone. She didn't seem to suffer any ill effects but she was very fat for a few days.

While all this was going on we had moved our church membership to a small mission closer to where we now lived. My Father had also moved to Hannibal, Mo. This little church was growing but slowly and we hoped to be of help there. It wasn't long till we realized the building was not big enough and we needed more space. The lot was long enough but not wide enough to build a building and have parking space available. One of the members was a carpenter and suggested we might be able to push the end of the building out and lengthen the auditorium. That idea caught on and in no time a support was put in to hold the roof in place while we tore out the west wall. We were left with room to continue meeting while the building went on. During that time the one who suggested that plan never seemed to be available to help and became a topic of not too friendly a discussion. After an evening of complaints we got the news that he had dropped dead of a ruptured aneurism. A sad time for some complainers that now felt they had wronged Bill.

My Father had moved to Hannibal and told the printer that did work for him that I was a printer pressman. He was in need of one and called me. I had been looking for a place to buy and have my own business and that call was very tempting. After some discussion we agreed it would be a good move. I notified Mr. Klene that I would come and he wanted me right away. Charlie Couts was not happy but I reminded him that I had been there for 13 years and had only one short vacation and deserved to go without further notice. He wasn't happy but gave me my final check before I left and thanked me for staying that long.

That one vacation was an exciting time for us, and the first time we had been out of the city in several years. I had just bought a new Rambler station wagon and it provided good transportation for the journey. Colorado Springs was the real stop on this trip and my grandmother and an aunt, on my mother's side, lived there. We visited with them and took them up to Garden of the Gods to picnic and drive around the park. Grandmother was very alert and when she heard my voice she said that must be JR. I had not seen her for fourteen years and she remembered that the last time we were together she wanted to spank me for using her flour to make paste for a kite. I had totally forgotten that ordeal.

From Colorado Springs we traveled on to Denver and visited the museum there then on to Yellowstone Park in Wyoming. The visit to the museum was interesting as we studied the dinosaur skeletons and other unusual things and spent the night in a motel. The trip to Yellowstone Park provided some time for the three children to get out and move around some. While mother was preparing a meal in the little cabin we rented Herby was out venturing around. He quietly said momma there is a bear here. When we looked out a bear was standing by the small porch to the cabin and he was a big one. Georgia was very frightened but the bear was only interested in the garbage can and not the boy. We visited the various geysers and started toward home the next day. Thinking there would be camping sites along the way we left in the evening and headed east but no camping sites were available anywhere along the way. I drove all night and stopped at a truck stop for a short nap and on toward home. During that night I was totally alone as all were asleep until I stopped and I was glad of it. I had traveled around Buffalo Bill Dam and it was a mess. The road was in repair and very rough and half of it was just mounted on the side of the cliff. I know Georgia would have been frightened at that sight. After driving for twenty one hours with only two hours sleep I was asleep within ten minutes after we arrived home.

Phase VIII
Move to Hannibal

I went on to Hannibal and stayed with Mother and Dad till I found an apartment, a duplex that was three stories high, and then went back and with help moved the family to that apartment. I began work there on Veterans Day and because it was a holiday. I received double-time-and-a-half for my first day at work. It was a union shop but because the newspaper had the most employees in that union they set the standard. Since it was necessary for the paper to go out the day after a holiday they had to work on those days so their contract only called for them to receive time-and-a-half for work on those days. Mr.

Klene expected the best work from his employees so he paid the extra pay. He was a great guy to work for. The majority of the work at Klene Printing was Law Briefs and had to be completed in a short time to meet the court dates. That often required us to work as much as 12 hours a day and sometimes more. It was hard working that required many hours but Mr. Klene worked right along with us and often brought coffee for us to keep us going. There was a tavern next door and often when the big cylinder press was running too fast the owner of the tavern would come over and tell us his glasses were falling off the shelf. That press was a 42" Babcock and as the bed of it went back and forth it even made the press jump back and forth and that made the tavern wall shake. We had four presses there and only one was an offset press. Several years later I visited Hannibal and found Jim, Mr. Klenes' son, had sold all the equipment and was now a printing broker in that same old building.

I don't know why but it seems God gave me some special ability to work on machines and diagnose problems in them. The largest press at Couts and Lantz was a 27x41 cylinder press with a Dexter feeder. It was a delicate thing to keep adjusted to feed the paper right. A year after I left there and moved to Hannibal, Missouri to work for Klene Printing I received a call from Charlie to tell the new pressman how to get it to work. I felt it was a compliment but also felt like telling him to read the manual. Of course the manual didn't exist. The work at Klene consisted of a weekly school paper, a weekly union paper and many law briefs. The law briefs were always in a hurry because they had to be in court at a certain time. As a result we were required to work many long hours to finish some and have them ready for delivery on time. Twelve hour days were common.

One young man was bringing paper up on the elevator and thought pulling the rope was too slow. So he grabbed the rope and jumped down the elevator pulling the rope and realized you have to pull the rope a long way to get the elevator to move three feet. In other words he just jumped down three stories of the elevator. He was bruised but mostly embarrassed.

Mr Klene had two sons but neither of them worked at the shop except on occasion when extra help was needed. Dave the youngest was pretty smart and wise but Jim was very reckless and often a problem for the Klene's who were great people. On one occasion he took his fathers' boat for a ride on the Mississippi river and somehow turned it over and it sank. Someone witnessed it and as they tried to rescue him he was holding the rope on the boat and wouldn't turn loose. They had to drag him and the boat to shore together because he new his dad would kill him if he didn't get the boat back. He was very drunk at the time.

The Missouri Baptist Men held a rally in Hannibal in 1957 and I was able to attend. I met Walter Harrington at the rally and found he was the manager of Missouri Baptist Press in Jefferson City. I had worked for him in Kansas City, at the Central Baptist Seminary, and helped run the Kansas Baptist Paper. He informed me that there was an opening at Baptist Press and asked if I would be interested in moving. Dr. Harding would have to approve it but he was there also if he could be found. After some questions from the two of them it was approved and I soon informed Mr. Klene I would like to make the change and he was glad to allow me to leave since I would be working with my own denomination. He was Catholic but very gracious.

Hannibal was located along the Mississippi River and a lake existed north of town that was where the river once ran. It had become sort of a resort area and people had put up cottages along the banks. It was a popular place to fish and my son Dick and I often went there to try our luck when I had a little time to spare. We have never been very good at luck but this one time we thought we had it made after Dick caught a nice catfish that probably weighed about 5 lbs. We put it on a good stringer and put it back in the water to continue to catch more. Well the more never showed up so we picked up the stringer to retrieve the fish and found only the head. It seems the turtles lived there too and they were also hungry. One of the staff at Hannibal LaGrange College, Woodrow Moore was a pilot and though I had not flown for several years he talked me into renewing my license and go flying with him. My interest in flying was renewed and I rented the small plane there and flew several times but it was getting expensive. I did fly some later with the CAP in Jeff City.

My Father remained at Calvary Church in Hannibal for 13 or 14 years and the church had grown from an attendance of 150 to over 600. The church had grown till it needed more space. The growth was not just from Dads preaching but from his compassion and desire to see people find Christ and life without fear and guilt. When he started his ministry there he tried to visit every home in the community and get thoroughly acquainted with them as a friend. That compassion did not stop with him but became infectious and every member of the church got involved. The Holy Spirit works through those who are compassionate and caring. That is real ministering and what God sent His followers to do.

Phase IX
The Move to Jefferson City

My last day to work for Mr. Klene was May 31 and I was paid for working on the holiday. Moving to Jefferson City was to require my going first and look for a place to live. I was invited to stay in the home of Dr. Allison until I could find a place and that only took a few days. I found a large house on Dunklin Street and soon went back to Hannibal to retrieve my family.

A local mover was recommended to move us and they went to Hannibal to meet me and quickly began to load every thing on the truck and it was soon very full. The last thing was a tabletop that I prized and it looked impossible. However the 'head man' took over and got it in the truck by 'slinging' it over the top very recklessly. I didn't appreciate that. The trip to Jeff City was not bad but it rained most of the way and a carpet and linoleum that they had tied on the outside of the truck was destroyed. It was good to get in and get settled but that old house was very breezy when winter came around and required a few extra covers.

We discovered much later that a box or two were missing and it was too late to find them. One contained an old family Bible that was an heirloom and we were sad at loosing it. Photographs we had taken on our only vacation were in one of those boxes as well as some from the flood of nineteen fifty one.

The work at the Baptist Press was great and variable as I expected. My experience before had covered all aspects of printing and I think I was prepared for it. Mr. Harrington was a fine man to work for and I appreciated his inviting me there. The Word and Way, Missouri Baptist newspaper was being printed and was the major part of the work. The type was set on a linotype machine and made into forms to print on the big cylinder press and required about three days to complete. It was folded and mailed in the mailroom on the second floor, to MBC churches all over the state. Other work included books of reports for associations, stationary and envelopes for churches, tracts and promotional material for various meetings of the convention. On my arrival at the Baptist Press there were three presses in operation but the offset was not too good. As time went by additional machines were added and a larger offset press was obtained with which we could print posters and the Children's Home Paper as well as being able to print booklets for associations from around the state and some from out of state. The staff there was made up of all Christian people and they were nice to be working with. I can't pass up the story of one of the staff that was very efficient and typed very fast and with almost no errors. She would be typing and at the same time listening to a recipe on the radio then stop typing long enough to write it down. One of the other typists would tell her to quit being so smart and making them look bad. Gip smith was the main operator of the big press and was responsible for getting the Word and Way printed. He had already retired from another job but worked at the Baptist press till he had to retire again for health reasons. We were printing the Children's Home paper monthly and on one occasion Woody Moore that had moved to work for them rented a plane in St. Louis and flew to Jefferson City to pick up the papers. I was sure it was too big a load for that Cesna but He insisted and got off the ground and safely to Bridgeton with the papers.

A lot of my time was spent helping the pressmen keep the presses running. The pressmen seemed to think as the old proverb that 'if anything can go wrong it will'. I have found the problem is a simple thing that can be easily fixed. 'If it works don't fix it' is always a good answer to those problems.

Jefferson City had several interesting places to visit but you can only see these so many times before they get boring. It became challenging to see other things so we began to check out the state parks. Missouri has many such attractions and some with lakes, rivers and caves. Round Springs was a very interesting place with a large camping area and of course the large spring. The stream running from the spring was very cold but many people waded or swam in it a short distance from the spring where it was not as cold. With hiking trails and many things to see it was an excellent place to relax. We visited several such parks and enjoyed the quiet and peace of them.

About three years after arriving in Jefferson City we were able to buy a nice house on Pierce Street just two blocks from our church. It had a nice yard and was large enough to accommodate the six of us. We had a nice yard for the kids to play in and a nice dry basement where they could play in bad weather.

We attended Calvary Baptist Church from the time we arrived in Jefferson City and enjoyed a great fellowship. We had attended there about two years and were visited by a friendly fellow that invited us to his church. Without hesitation Georgia asked which church he attended. When he said Calvary Baptist Georgia, without a thought, said that's where we go and I don't remember seeing you there. He was obviously embarrassed and we never did see him in church.

A few short years went by and space became a necessity for a high chair for a new baby, Rose. The kitchen was a kitchen and dining room combined and not big enough for any addition. A search for something bigger began and a small farm about five miles west on Route C was perfect. Ten rooms, four bedrooms and a large kitchen seemed the perfect solution. Three acres for the kids to run on and some space for a garden was now in our hands. Some difficulties arose there as the kids had many after school activities that made transportation a problem. We went through three cars while living there and Dick got a car of his own that helped with rides. After a few years we decided it would be more practical to live in town and a search began again.

A number of interesting things happened while we lived on the little farm but none fatal. Herb pulled the lawn mower over his foot and sliced the top off his shoe and came in to tell his mother it was all right just the shoe was hurt. I think she almost fainted until he pulled off the shoe to show her the toe was still there. Rose was very young then and staying home with mother but old enough to explore. One evening she was missing and friends and neighbors joined to look for her. She was found only a few feet from the house but in the brush where she had laid down to take a nap.

During the time I worked at Missouri Baptist Press I had become acquainted with Don Beck when he needed help with his Triumph sports car. I worked with him on other cars but he came to me after we moved to Indian Meadow Drive and introduced me to a young man that had a Volvo that was in a mess. He had taken it to a trade school to be worked on and rebuilt and someone messed up big. The cylinders had been bored too large and the new pistons were too small. After a look at the catalog from which the new parts had been ordered I found they listed oversize pistons for the car and returned the pistons for exchange. It was necessary to bore the cylinders slightly but the wrist pin was too large and the rods had to be rebored to fit. Charles was happy to see his car in operation again and this was the beginning of many years of working on antique and classic cars for his dad. A 1937 Cord appeared in my back yard and soon the owner and I were working on it to get it ready to go to Auburn Indiana for the auto show there where the Cord, Auburn and Dusenberg were built. It was a beautiful automobile and required some miner work to get it polished and ready to show. It had some features that were very new and different and soon required some special work. The starter was operated by a special system that had a "startex" that would engage the starter but would disengage when he engine started. It was activated by the clutch and had to disengage for shifting gears. The gears were operated by a vacuum system that was controlled by a small switching system on the steering column.

Soon my parking area was the parking place for a 1951 Rolls Royce that needed a lot of work as well as a 1956 Mercedes and a 1937 Henry J Kaiser. The Mercedes needed valve work and the Henry J needed much body work as well as repainting. These cars all belonged to a well known Surgeon that collected them in hopes of being able to sell them at a profit and use the money for medical mission work over seas. The profit diminished after he got the Cord out of a very damp basement garage to drive to the hospital and since it had no defroster managed to drive broadside into a pickup truck. That was 30 years ago and the Cord is still not on the road. I don't know the demise of the other cars but the Cord is near ready to be finished.

I worked at the Missouri Baptist Press for twenty years and enjoyed every year but the financial arrangements were not to my liking. Mr. Harrington resigned after my fifteenth year and I was asked to serve as Director of the press. Most of my efforts to improve the operation were wasted because the finances were handled by the bookkeeping staff of the Baptist Building and not our staff. As a result the records indicated we were losing money when in fact we were making a profit. After five years as director the idea of moving the Press to the Baptist Building so the present building could be sold was presented to me. I did not like the arrangement proposed so I resigned so some one else could have the honors of making the move. I was not really ready to retire but I had fallen behind on work at home and I knew the Lord would provide. For a few months I worked around the house and finished a few projects and dug moles out of the yard. That summer I dug out 16 moles by standing and waiting for them to move so I could see where they were and dig them out with a hoe. They had made a mess of the yard.

While we were still on the farm I drove a very small car called a BMW Isetta. The only door was the front of the car and the rear wheels were set close together so it looked like a three-wheeler. It had a one cylinder BMW motorcycle engine behind the only seat. With four-speed transmission it got very good mileage and was fun to drive. One problem arose when my RA boys wanted to go somewhere and there were six of them. It was not wise but we made it. My daughter Gladys and I were in the Civil Air Patrol at the time and we used it a few times to travel as far as Versailles in searches. The CAP had a Piper Cup tandem seat plane for search missions and I was able to fly it in a few missions before some smart kids decided to steal the engine out of it. Before the engine was stolen a fellow member wanted to go for a ride so we took off and headed for Hannibal, MO. I had taken a thermos of coffee and ask Joe Bewig, the passenger to pour me a little coffee. Without hesitation he removed the cap and was struck with shock as the coffee came out like a column and immediately went straight back in without spilling a drop. He immediately decided I didn't need coffee.

When we arrived at the airport in Hannibal the updrafts were so strong I had to land with almost full throttle to get the plane down. On one interesting occasion a fellow employee wanted to go for a ride in a plane so at lunch hour they were willing to give up lunch and go fly. Joyce, Bobbie B, and Bob got in the plane, that I had to rent, and took off for a short ride over town.

The weather looked great until we got in the air and I could see to the north a very heavy storm moving our way. I didn't want to get caught in that so I quickly headed for the field where the windsock indicated a south wind and was on the last leg to land when suddenly the plane gained about 50 miles an hour without added power. The storm had already hit and the wind was strong and the rain heavy. It was too late to do anything but do a 180 degree turn and land to the north instead. It was a very steep and sudden turn in which the plane went to a 90 degree bank but no one seemed to be bothered by it and we landed safely but wet. Herb got his first plane ride in a Cesna plane I rented and I let him try to fly it and he was quite young. He pulled back on the stick and we went into a steep climb then he pushed forward on it and put us into a steep dive. He thought that was fun but he ends up flying hot air balloons.

By this time our family had grown to a real crowd and by 2000 it was difficult to get them all together. On Christmas of 2004 all of the family, except four were present for celebration and a photo was taken and the missing were added in by computer.

Thirty-three Herifords All Together

During my years at Missouri Baptist Press we were members at Calvary Baptist Church and involved in almost every activity. Georgia had a great interest in missions and worked in WMU and the GAs. GAs was the girls' organization of the WMU and she spent a lot of time working with them and enjoyed it greatly. I was soon elected as a deacon and trustee and also worked with the boys' organization. We enjoyed all of the work but it did take a lot of our time. All of our children were involved in those groups until they grew up.

Calvary Church had many difficulties that came about because of misunderstanding and then distrust. As a result pastors didn't stay very long and the problem did not go away. One pastor served that was very different and compassionate. As a result the church grew until the auditorium was full at every service. He felt the church should build a bigger building and some felt the building should stay where it was to minister to that community. It could become possible in the future to buy property next door to expand, and it did later on but not in time for what was about to take place. The church was divided on the subject and soon was totally divided to the point that half started another church. That became a difficult time in the life of the church and it was to affect it for time to come. One pastor was very eager and the church took in over one hundred new members in one year. There was a problem that again hurt the church because that pastor was getting people to join but they never came back. In fact the average attendance fell during his ministry. The culmination of his ministry was exiting as on his last message he talked of his new assignment as being with lawyers and doctors and etc. and he was thrilled to be working with a higher class of people. Talk about a slap in the face!

The GA group Georgia worked with received a quarterly magazine that always had requests for volunteers to go to mission stations around the world to help missionaries. In one such magazine was a request for a printer. Georgia felt my experience was just what was needed and wrote to the Mission Board and asked for more information. We filled out papers and sent them in only to find out they did not send volunteers that had teenagers at home. That put the idea out of our minds for the time but not for long. I will return to that later.

Dick joined the navy while we lived on the little farm on Route C on July 27, 1967 and on May 11, 1968 was married to Marcia Renee Ehler. She was a sweet young lady but liked home and didn't stay away very long at a time. After Dick finished boot camp at the Great Lakes he transferred to Japan. That was quite a distance for them to be separated and Dick got to the point at which he could get permission for her to come to Japan so they could be together. I have often wondered if it took much begging on Dicks' part to get her to start that way and I think she wondered why she started after she got to Tokyo. For a homebody girl she was very brave and the trip was successful but not without unnerving experiences. The plane she left Washington on was Japanese and no one spoke English. When she arrived in Tokyo, timing with landing erred and she had to sit for an hour or so and again no one spoke English and she didn't know what to do. Dick finally arrived and things worked out but I think she was a brave lady. They now have two sons, a daughter and four sweet granddaughters.

During all the things and places of the past Georgia has remained a faithful mother and home maker but with the children growing up and some thinking of going off to college and the service she felt a need for something more to do. She enrolled in a class for License Practical Nursing. It meant a lot of hard work and study but she persevered and graduated and applied for a license to practice. She soon found work in a nursing home and then in the hospital and she enjoyed helping people. This experience would later prove to be of value in another way. This however added to the problems which every home eventually may face, as the need for transportation for school children became a problem. It seems every child wants to be involved in extra activities and it required extra miles of driving. The 1963 rambler we had driven ever since leaving Hannibal had accumulated a lot of miles. We considered buying another but funds did not come available easily so we were determined to get by. One day Georgia was taking kids to a GA meeting and just dropped them off and was returning home when a fellow whose license had expired and had bad eyes met her at an intersection at the same time and the rambler was tossed on its top. The damage was very serious and Georgia was bruised but she was able to continue working though very disturbed. Not because of her injuries but because of the thought that it could have happened while kids were in the car. Seat belts were not a requirement as yet and that made it a frightening experience for her.

The side of the car was caved in very bad but I managed to push it out with hydraulic help and we continued to drive it till we could manage something else. That something else turned out to be a Volkswagon Van and served us for some time but the engine had to be replaced twice and I gave up and traded it the only way I could afford. That became expensive as the Pontiac I traded for had a huge engine in it and the many trips to town became too much to bear. We had enjoyed the time on the little farm but with Georgia driving to town and running the kids to so many activities we were going broke. A search for a home became a necessity again. A fairly new house became available soon so we investigated and thanks to a realtor that wanted to buy our old house we were able make a deal and prepared to move again. The next move was made in March and of course there had to be one more snow that year and on the day we planned to move.

While we lived on the farm several interesting things took place. The need for pets seemed to be important so a dog was found that became an important part of our lives for quiet awhile but a goat was added to the collection. That little goat was much too smart and caused quite a stir. The house had a double garage, which I made good use of, and it had a breezeway about 15 feet wide between the house and garage. It was enclosed and had glass on both ends that made a nice play area in bad weather. That goat found out how to open the door and get into the breezeway and get to her food. The problem arose when I opened the door and tried to get her out and she didn't like the door but jumped through the window instead. I had to replace three windows before we decided the goat had to go. That goat was Gladys' friend and to see her go was not easy. An ad was put in the paper and a buyer came soon to see her. That would have been fine except the buyer had to say the goat would make good barbeque. That hurt Gladys tremendously and she and her mother didn't get along very good for a while.

Throughout our lives we have entertained pets of many kinds. On the farm in Kansas City, Kansas two black Labrador mix dogs became good pets. They loved the farm and being able to run free. They were also very excited to see us return from church or town. A young man I worked with needed somewhere to park his mobile home so I let him park it near our house and gave him one of the dogs. They moved out of town and took that dog with them but we had the other to guard the house while we were away. After being offered a good price for the farm we moved to town but about a year later went to visit the family that had moved into that house. To our surprise that dog recognized us even in a different car and came running to jump into the car and climb all over the kids he had been missing.

I mentioned the burrow before but she was an exciting pet and all will remember her.

When we moved to Hannibal in 1956 we took a blond spaniel with us and had difficulty keeping him from chasing cars and people walking by. He was a cute dog and good company for the boys but began to have eye trouble. He continued to chase cars and we soon realized he was totally blind as he walked around the house after someone had moved chairs and walked into the moved chairs. He finally failed a car chasing and was hit by one and killed.

In Jefferson City we acquired a terrier that became a close pet and was very little trouble. When we moved to the farm on Route C he went along and enjoyed the freedom there. The boys had grown a lot and paid little attention to him but he was faithful and followed us to Indian Meadow Drive. I had mentioned the goat before but we also had cats there on the farm. It seemed to be a good place to dump unwanted animals and two yellow cats appeared that were pretty and cuddlesome but also mischievous. They tried to climb the curtains, the walls and people if they stood too still. They survived but became outdoor cats.

The terrier remained with us at Indian Meadow drive and cats seem to show up but became a problem as new kittens were born. A male cat nearby tore the screen off the back door and got in to kill the kittens. That brought tears and anger but cats have their nature and it is hard to change that. An uncle gave us a male Schnauzer puppy which we didn't need but became a major attraction. He was very emotional and barked at every one that came to the door. One lady and her husband never liked him because he never stopped barking when they came to visit. When others came to visit he would stop barking as soon as they greeted him but not so with the Johnsens'. I will never know why but it was puzzling. When we left for Malawi our daughter took care of him until he died. When we left for Malawi our granddaughter gave us a stuffed Schnauzer to take along that looked very real and some of the missionaries said we couldn't keep a pet in the apartment. Then they realized it was fake.

At our fiftieth wedding anniversary our son Mark brought us a two year old Schnauzer that a family had to get rid of and he became a very close pet and friend until he had to be put to sleep fifteen years later. He also traveled with us and was no trouble while traveling. Gladys lived next door to us and had cats most of the time. One female cat she offered to her mother and she was a real pet. She was house broken and cuddly and was good company. A certain song I liked to sing seemed to have some effect on her and she would climb up on my lap and look right at my mouth as if to see where it was coming from. Maybe she was trying to tell me to stop. Georgia was having trouble with allergies and was afraid it was the cat so when Gladys moved to Arkansas she took "Effie' with her.

Since Georgia died I have not had a pet but have had plenty to do without one.

I had been doing most of the work on our cars for some time and after purchasing the new 55 Rambler while in KC and finding the mechanics couldn't get it to start right. I decided I could do as well and from there on I lost faith in others working on my car. The family we had purchased the little farm from, had a teenage son with a small car that I think was an Aronda. He was having trouble with it and came to me for help. That was to start a new challenge for me that involved working on other cars for friends. He later had a Triumph sports car and it offered a lot of experiences. Later he was to introduce me to another friend that became a steady customer. I'll return to that story later.

The move was not hindered much and we now had a nice home that was closer to work and our church. By now Dick was in the navy and Gladys had gone to Central Missouri University and now to Missouri University. We soon found a nice house with three bedrooms, a nice living room, a kitchen-dinning room that proved to be the perfect place for us. With Gladys gone off to college and Dick in the navy Rose had her own room and the two boys had a room so Georgia and I had a room to ourselves. It had a full basement with part of it divided off for a garage where I could work on cars and etc. The yard was large and had cherry trees and a nice place for a garden. Except for a year Georgia and I spent in Malawi that was our home until 1988.

Gladys was studying art and decided to go to Arizona to study. She called me at work one day and said she was moving to Arizona and I told her we needed to talk about it and she should come home and discuss it. Without hesitation she said no she was loaded up and on her way and would call us later. That didn't go over with her Mother very well and Georgia became very worried and frustrated about it. It was quite some time before we heard from her and that worried Georgia more but the worst was yet to come. When we did hear from her it was a greater shock to her mother and to her grandmother as they both had a habit of worrying. She had decided to move to Florida and there was a huge hurricane moving that way. Georgia and her Mother continued to worry and fret until I told them they had prayed about it so it was time to leave it to the Lord. Gladys made the move without incident and survived.

In 1970 we received a call from KC saying Georgia's Mother had passed away. It was a surprise because her mother had not been sick. She apparently just went to sleep and didn't wake up. The 1963 Rambler we were driving at the time had a lot of miles and was rather noisy so Herb had bought a Volkswagon Bug and he drove Georgia to Kansas City to be with family while I tried to find a better car. I stopped in the Fiat dealers and ended up buying a new 1970 Fiat. I find it hard to believe I was able to buy a new car then at $1900.00 and that same car today would cost over $25,000. I made it to the funeral on time and the new car was nice to travel in. It made a rather hasty trip soon after when Gladys did finally call us from Florida to inform us she was expecting soon. That was disturbing to her Mother but we had to drive to Ft. Lauderdale to see her and our first granddaughter. The new one was very cute and we wanted to bring her home then but Gladys wanted to stay there and come back on her own which she did quite well. She was living in an apartment but later purchased a 15 foot camper trailer to return with. She had a 1955 Datsun to pull it with but it managed.

Gladys decided to go back to Arizona and pulled that camper trailer there with the Datsun. I don't know how she survived but she did until someone stole her car. It was later found in Denver, Colorado and they wanted $150 dollars to retrieve it. In the mean time Herb had finished school and felt sorry for Gladys in her struggle in Arizona and packed up his guitar and walked half a mile from home on a very cold night to hitchhike to be with her. The two of them got to Denver some how and with money I sent them retrieved the car and returned home without a hood on the car. The car was in bad shape and plugs in bad shape so she managed to get a 55 Chevy truck on which we built a cabin for her to travel in. It was a very solid cabin and also very heavy.

We decided to make a trip to North Carolina to visit my brother so Gladys loaded her truck with the necessary things and Georgia and I loaded the Fiat and a little trailer I had built and Rose, Mark and little Heather headed for the East. We got caught in heavy rains before we got to Cape Girardeau and couldn't get to the camping site for the night so tried to sleep in Gladys' truck and in the Fiat. We soon learned the camper was not leak proof and all blankets as well as people got soaked. The next day we headed East, but found many roads under water and had to take 'diversions' to get on our way. Having passed that we were making good time until the truck threw a rod bearing. A Tennessee park was not far away so we managed to get to it and ended up camping there for a week while I took the engine apart and put in a new crankshaft and bearings there in the park.

In 1978 I resigned at Missouri Baptist press after 20 years there. After a few weeks I went to work for the Missouri Education Association, where Gladys had been working, for printing the materials they used in working with teachers all over Missouri. A Multilith offset that was an automatic machine that made the plates, a copying system that inserted them on the press and printed the number required. Manuscripts placed in the hopper were fed in automatically so it was a matter of keeping the machine clean and watching for troubles to occur. It was a part-time job but sufficient for the time and soon became full-time or nearly so. I worked for them for some time and enjoyed the work and staff but was shocked when I heard the language some of the women used. For some reason they seemed to sense I was different and when I entered a room where they were talking the language changed. I hoped that would change some things but I don't know the outcome.

Phase X
Invitation to Malawi

It was while I worked at MNEA that we received a call from the Foreign Mission Board wanting to know if our status had changed so we might be able to consider a mission trip.

We had almost forgotten the idea but were glad to consider it again. Some of the questions we faced included money, what to do with our home while we were gone, and how to handle our finances at home? We did respond and were sent papers to sign and a request for our personal experience with God. A few days after we returned the papers a letter requesting we meet with a representative that would be in Jefferson City for another meeting. That took place very soon and we were encouraged but still had no idea of how to finance the occasion. We had expressed our concern to the representative so we were hoping something could be worked out. A few days passed by but soon we had a request to meet in Richmond, Virginia to learn more. Our expectations were that we were going to learn more and had made no plans to pack up and go. We were a little surprised to find out plans had already been made for our trip and they were waiting for us to set a date. That was a bit of a shock but not one that hurt because by now we were convinced it was in Gods plan for us. We had studied missions and prayed for missions so it must be our turn to get involved in missions.

The next few weeks were busy ones as we made arrangements for the house, which worked out well, and for our finances to be taken care of by our son Dick. It seems our kids were glad to see us go. Not because they wanted us gone but because they knew of our concern for missions. We had been without family at home for some time now and were ready for a more challenging life and they must have recognized it. The date for leaving was set and tickets arrived and now we realized it had really come to pass. What do you pack for a years travel away from home and in a foreign country? A lot! The kids had bought us two large suitcases and we had two from other travels. With those and a few small handbags we felt we had enough and we did survive but later wished we had brought other things. Film was not easy to get there unless someone was going to South Africa but we had taken several rolls so we were comfortable with that. The camera we had taken disappeared at the airport in Amsterdam and we were without for awhile but with a phone call and the 'postal service' we soon had another and were ready for it because we were seeing so many things that we wanted to be able to remember. We left the local airport and flew to St. Louis to catch a plane to Chicago where we caught a KLM plane to go to Amsterdam. The flight was fine except for the time lapse that seemed weird to us. We had taken off at 5 and were fed the evening meal immediately. That was OK since we had no food for a while but just two hours later they came bringing us breakfast. Our stomachs had not finished with the other meal yet. Following that feeding the lights were lowered and a movie was started on a large screen to the front of that section of the plane. We had not slept for near 24 hours and wanted to take a nap but that wasn't to happen. We just could not fall asleep because the hours were messed up for us. Just two hours later another meal was on the way and we had had all we could take for the day.

We were glad to arrive in Amsterdam and get to move around a little and we had a six-hour lay over. A hotel was provided for us to rest but we still could not sleep so we took a tour of Amsterdam on the local bus and walked around Dam Square and took some pictures but it was rainy and cloudy and the pictures didn't come out good at all. I had finished that roll and had it in my pocket or we never would have known what they were like for the camera disappeared as we entered the next plane to Nairobi, Kenya. Georgia was shocked as we walked down the street heading for Ann Franks' apartment and the street was lined with prostitutes and porn sites. Girls were standing in the doors waving at men or women to come in.

We had a very short layover in Nairobi and changed planes to go to Blantyre, Malawi and we were required to take care of our luggage during that time. We learned later that was not supposed to be but it gave some unscrupuless workers a chance to swindle you out of your dollars. The trip to Blantyre was shorter but we got a nice look at the famous Kilamonjaro Mountain that I think is Africas highest.

Our arrival in Blantyre occurred at about 11 pm and we were met there by Jerry Spires to help us get through customs and immigration. That was an interesting time for us, and a young Malawian that inspected our luggage. I had taken my Diawa fishing rod with me and had it curled around in one of our big cases. When he unzipped it the rod flew out and he about fell over with fright. I was told later that Jerry was surprised the guard had not warned us about such things. Jerry took us to the mission compound and showed us to a nice little apartment and helped us arrange our luggage for a temporary stay since we would soon be going to Lilongwe, the capital. By the time Jerry left us it was midnight but our bodies thought it was only 2 in the afternoon. It was still difficult to get to sleep but in four hours I had slept some but was ready to get out and survey my new surroundings. I quickly dressed and stepped outside to see a beautiful world. Flowers were everywhere and there was a beautiful aroma that I had never experienced. As I walked around looking at the wonders I had just been blessed with I discovered a tree with amazing blooms and a sweet aroma. As I got closer I realized the tree didn't smell sweet up close at all. In fact it was a little nauseous. Then I realized that tree was the source of the aroma in the whole area. I was still groggy from jet lag and loss of sleep but awake enough to enjoy Gods world.

Sunday morning and we learned our apartment was the meeting place for the adult Sunday School class and we had to clean it up a bit. A joy was to appear when we were to meet some of the nicest people with whom we were to be working. The apartment was on the mission compound and services were held in an auditorium there near our apartment. That Sunday morning we enjoyed hearing some joyful people singing with gladness in their own language and it was beautiful. This was going to be a great experience for us and it had just begun. The next morning Jerry Spires picked us up with our luggage and we headed up the Kamusa highway to Lilongwe. Then came our introduction to things we had seen in movies but thought that was from a long time ago.

Bible Study in Small Village

Not so, because people were still living in small mud brick huts with grass roofs and those were gathered in groups that in some cases numbered in the hundreds.

So much can be said about our journey to Africa that I know I would leave out the best but I feel our journey will not be complete until it is shared to the best of my ability.

The entire country was beautiful and the people were also. The trees that bloom so gorgeously, the aroma that floated to your nostrils so continuously, the friendliness of the people all added up to real beauty. Lilongwe was about 150 miles from Blantyre but the time on the trip went by fast as we absorbed what we were to see for the next year. Both Blantyre and Lilongwe were large cities and I wouldn't guess how large but we were to get to know Lilongwe very well. We were taken to the mission compound there and placed in a nice brick apartment that was in a fenced yard. We soon learned that all yards were fenced and some with walls that had broken glass imbedded in the top to deter thieves from climbing them. This meant that not all Malawians were righteous. All we met were very gracious, helpful and generous. All of them were so pleased at learning new things that every morning at work a new 'prizy' (gift) was on my desk.

After meeting Barbara Workman and with her generosity and helpfulness we were able to rest a bit and venture about the grounds and learn more of our surroundings. The more we saw the more we praised the Lord for this assignment. That evening we were invited to the home of the Workman's for dinner and to meet the officers and pastors of the Malawi convention. That was a very difficult evening for us as our body clocks told us it was time to sleep and we could hardly stay awake to eat let alone visit. The Workman's were very hospitable and tried hard to make us comfortable in our new surroundings.

Tuesday was a slow day and we did relax a bit but Gerald Workman took me to the publishing house to introduce me to the staff and equipment. Barbara Workman introduced Georgia to the markets and how to get around in this very different town. The staff was supposed to be on holiday but they came in to meet me. December is a holiday for them so they can get corn planted for the family. Rains usually start sometime in November or December and they need to get the seed in the ground as soon as the rains arrive to get the best crops. I had most of the month to look things over and fix a few machines but some of the staff wanted to be there to help so I was not alone. The repair work didn't get far since I didn't know all the problems but I learned as soon as work began that the Heidleberg press needed major work and money was needed for that. The Multilith had been wrecked and I spent a lot of time rebuilding the delivery unit on it. The delivery bars had been damaged by something being dropped in where it didn't belong and straightening them took some time. When the staff returned they were shocked to see it run and at a speed they didn't know it could attain. The Heidleberg would work but not good. It needed new rollers and a lot of clean up and since a friend had sent money to my account I was able to order 4 new rollers which took some time to get there from South Africa. I soon learned that the staff was definitely untrained and felt for a while that this trip was a mistake. I decided that if God could get me over there He could take care of the rest as well and that He did.

We were introduced to Lilongwe Baptist Church across town from our apartment but near where several of the staff lived. Reverend Chisi was the pastor then and he had a wife and several children. The Church building was not very large but the congregation was. Sunday School was well attended and children met out in the yard while the adults met inside with women on one side and men on the other. Each had a different teacher and we expected the division then but we soon learned that the congregation sat that way all the time. So Georgia sat with the women on the right side and I sat with the men on the other. The two sides were separated by about ten feet and the children sat on the floor in the center. Bambo Chisi was a great pastor and I enjoyed the services very much but Georgia was bothered by the fact that she could not understand Chichewa. More about the church later but now back to the shop.

The employees were members of different churches and all wanted us to visit their church. We did so eventually and enjoyed great hospitality. Some of the staff lived in distant villages and had to walk as much as nine miles to work. Some had bicycles and that became another unrelated task for me. I had the joy of helping them keep bicycles going. Tires were not a big problem as they just tied a knot on each side of a leak and went on riding.

We were provided a Volkswagon Golf to drive and informed we might be expected to provided transportation for Malawians to various meetings and they would show us how to get to the right place. They knew the way because they had walked there before. That posed a problem for us at first since the way they walked sometimes didn't look like a road. We never failed to get through. Roads were not like here in Missouri but they were sufficient for walking and that fit their needs. Roads to villages often were paths that ran through other villages, sometimes several villages. It was as if we drove through yards to get to the next yard. I would get totally lost if some one of them were not with me. At least no one sued us for wrecking their yard.

The real joy of the work there was in hearing them sing as they worked and the songs they sang were usually our favorite hymns. They were happy people and being as poor as they were and being happy made me feel so rich and yet humble to see that money was not what made life worth enjoying.

Ngnombeyoyera's church was near by and yet very rural. As soon as we drove off the tarmac road it became a narrow path not designed for cars. The church was small and had only openings for windows. The door was low and some of us had to duck (or bow) to enter. Bow to enter the house of God. How appropriate. There were no pews but someone brought a chair so the speaker could set down and the rest sat on the floor. Georgia was always very prominent with white hair and light complexion setting in the middle of all the ladies. I spoke about tithing that day and pointed out that tithing was not just about money but all of life. David Kamvabingo served as my interpreter and I only hope he was repeating what I said and not another subject of his choosing.

I would later attend my first native funeral in that village and visited there often to transport the sick to the hospital. I was invited to speak at several churches and enjoyed it very much because the people were so courteous and generous. It was expected for us to eat at one of the homes and we enjoyed the fellowship and the generosity. Even when they had so little and we had plenty they wanted to treat you for being there. A few times we had to eat at more than one home and we would be overstuffed. The food they served was always nsima with a relish of meat or vegetable and it was always good. The nsima was corn flour they had pounded themselves from the grain they had raised and it was cooked in water till the water was fully absorbed leaving a stiff mush. The relish was cooked with onion, salt, tomato and curry powder and the nsima was picked from the bowl by fingers and dipped in the relish for seasoning. We have cooked some for friends to try and I just bought some corn flour to try to do so again but I had to settle for yellow corn flour since no one seems to carry white here. We never served the entrals with ours but they are never in the chickens we buy now days. They always tasted as good as any other part of it since they were cooked with the same seasoning.

We always felt bad about driving to the village because they had to walk all the time. Some as much as nine miles and that would have me tired before I got to work. When we went to a village the people seemed to know whom we would visit so they would run around to other homes and find two chairs for us to sit down. Most of them just sat on the ground to eat or talk but wanted visitors to feel comfortable.

I could never remember all the materials we printed but a lot of it was for the Bible School that was located on the compound. Some seminary materials were part of the work and stationary for the missionaries. We printed several tracts and literature and in several languages. Chichewa, Tumbuka and Yao I remember but there may have been more. Translation was a problem as the missionaries wanted nationals to do it so it would be more like they used the language. However, some did not know the entire English grammar well enough to put it into their grammar. A lot of checking had to be done to make sure each translation was correct. I was glad I didn't have to be responsible for that even though I did learn some of the language. I can only remember some of the people we knew there but most of the staff I can. The names may be odd to some but some had great meaning. One that helped keep the building clean was Ngombeyoyera, which meant white cow. That got him the nickname of holy cow. Others were simpler as Bambo Monde. Bambo was the term for father or mister. Mayi was the term for mother or Misses. If the man was not married he was not Bambo even if he was an old boy. Mayi Pumila was the typist, Mayi Ladd was a bindery worker, Bambo Bornwell a pressman. Bambo Gnosi the cook and lawn keeper. He was also the champion Bawo player. That was a popular game played by many and often for gambling. Ngombeyoyera was the first to invite me to his church and it thrilled me to be invited not because I can preach but to get to know the people better.

Village Church

Many people go on tours to other countries but I had the privilege to tour their lives and culture and they were grateful and so was I. There are many that speak English and always someone to interpret and I enjoyed those visits each time. One thing that bothered me was the generosity of the people when I knew they had very little. You never visit a village where you were not expected to eat with them. We were told by the missionaries that we might be fed anything but it would be good to eat because it was always cooked very well. I can verify the fact that the entrails are as good as the heart. They really knew how to flavor things.

The churches in the villages were usually small and had openings but no windows or glass in them. I think the second church I visited was one in the mountains east of Lilongwe. I drove a Volkswagon Golf and that was needed for transport for a pastor and a deacon. That was a memorable experience as we drove this narrow mountain road and reached one point where the road was just the side of the mountain and the car tilted so we could see straight down the mountain. That was to be emphasized later as we left the church six hours later. The service had gone well and Bambo Chisi had finished the 70-

minute sermon and the plan was to walk to the creek, down the mountain, for baptismal service. The first rain of the season came just as we were ready to walk out and it was a downpour. It lasted for over an hour and someone came to say the creek was flooded so the next service would have to be postponed. The next step was to go on with the Lords supper and that could be done. At that moment a boy's choir that had been singing at another church and on their way home, dashed in to get out of the rain. The next hour we enjoyed some beautiful music as they entertained us. We did go on with the Lords supper and the rain stopped so we could load up to leave. The next thing that struck my mind was that spot where we drove along the side of the mountain at a grave angle. Would the Golf stay on the road or would it slide off? Thanks to the front wheel drive we made it although the rear wheels were farther down the mountain than the front. We made it and another day had been a joy. I am sure I will forget many things of interest but I hope the things I do remember and put in this story will be those that will relate to all who read it that the power and love of God is very great. I often thought of the story of Peter at Pentecost when all the people heard his message as though it were in their own language. As I sat in the services while Rev. Chisi preached in Chichewa I heard a great message as though it were in my English. The Holy Spirit was speaking in His language and all can understand that. God is so good.

Following the service I was asked to drive the pastor and deacons, that had gone along to the village, to a near by farm. It was not really near by but to them it was. We ended up taking a different route around the mountain and found the required farm very close to the road. A large banana orchard was visible but the citrus orchard they were looking for was out of sight. By walking several yards through the bananas we found the citrus orchard and it was beautiful. When we bought oranges at the market they were very sour because they were picked early before someone else stole them. These were perfect and the aroma was attractive even tough I never eat them. Each one found a bucket or box and began to fill it with choice oranges and lemon. I manage to get a few grapefruit but I felt bad not paying someone for them because they were great.

The Bible school was located on the same grounds as the publishing house and we had the privilege of knowing the staff there. Some of them were also members of Lilongwe Baptist Church where we attended weekly. Mayi Kalaka had a great voice and often highlighted the end of a chorus with a high trill that gave it a beautiful finish. Bambo Mulungo was a pastor and also a teacher in the Bible School and a fun fellow, He loved the Lord and also fun and fellowship. All of the missionaries participated in the teaching at the school and different ones served as leaders of it since at least one family was on furlough. I thoughally enjoyed the music at every church we attended for the people sang with such enthusiasm that it was almost heavenly. They sang out as though they really loved the Lord.

The members of the staff at the publishing house were all interesting people and I had the privilege of visiting in each of their homes and meeting their families. They were so gracious and always wanted to provide food and I didn't need it like they did. One individual that I remember as John was also a village preacher and loved to talk. So much so that at times the work was slowed down. On one occasion I walked in and as though I was turning the volume down, twisted a button on his shirt. All of them recognized the move and laughed but John just shut up and said nothing the rest of the day. That did not last more than a day though.

Bambo David Kamvibingo was the cameraman and lacked a lot as to knowledge of the process and required retraining so we had good negatives to work with. All of them were happy to learn new things and that made this whole story a real blessing. After each lesson there would be some 'prizy' on my desk the next morning. They wanted to learn all they could and wanted to express appreciation for it. David was no different but did prove to have other problems. He had four children and they were all very bright and courteous and wanted to wait on me every time I visited. David had hopes of getting 'up' in this world and began to use the supplies and equipment for his own purpose, nothing real serious but illegal none-the-less and was released. Getting people to understand that little errors are just as big in Gods eye as the worst crime anyone can commit is not easy. God is serious when He gives us orders and loves obedience. I guess I was privileged to name David's new baby and the name I gave them was John. All babies are cute but he was special since I had named him. The Malawians always kept a bucket of water in the house for cooking and drinking. Usually about five gallons and large enough that little John fell in and drowned. He was just starting to crawl around on his own.

I have said little about the food we were offered in the homes and I must relate something of it because it was good. Plenty of vegetables were available as well as fish, beef and chicken. Meat was cheap for us but to them it was expensive and necessitated buying a very small amount at a time since they had no refrigeration. The main food for them was the corn, which they could grow themselves. Usually that was not sufficient to last a whole year and they had to buy it either whole or ground to flour. Naturally the ground corn was more expensive and they would have to buy 200 pound bags of shelled corn and carry it home the best way they could. The corn was cooked in water with no seasoning until it was a very thick mush called nsima. That was served in a large lump to be dipped in a relish called 'ndiwo' that could be any kind of meat or vegetable that was seasoned with tomato, salt, onion and curry powder. Eating hot nsima with fingers was a new thing for us but we soon adapted and still enjoy fixing such a meal now. It was always delicious no matter what the relish. I don't remember being fed fish heads but that was the favorite of the head of the house as well as the chicken heads and feet. We did have goat entrails at one meal and that was as good as any.

Georgia and I each had the opportunity of traveling with one of the missionaries to distant parts of Malawi. Georgia went with Marlyn Upton on several ventures and one of those became a regular trip for her. Her training as a LPN was put to use when a pastor that had been injured on a bicycle had to have an injured leg treated regularly. It was in a cast that they had cut a hole in so an infection could be cleaned and treated. That part was fine but it meant traveling through several villages and to a remote one to treat him. The roads there were not avenues or boulevards but walking paths. You had to remember which path to take and Georgia feared she might get lost by herself but she made it fine and became more venturesome. She also traveled north to a town where no missionary was living but work was still going on for those that had become Christians. Georgia went with Rebecca Pfifer to NcotaNcota that was near the north end of lake Malawi. The mission had a home there where they could stay but no furniture. They had gone with sleeping bags to sleep on the floor but no protection from snakes or other varmints that might be there. They survived and had a good meeting and avoided the rainy season that would have made the trip impossible.

I made several trips to take pastors and laymen to various affairs and one was a real eye opener for me. This meeting was held in a remote village where a tobacco auction barn was located and a large parking area became a perfect spot for a revival meeting. It was Friday evening when we arrived and began to set up a screen, film projector and a PA system. A generator provided the power and a few lights were hung to give a little light so villagers could see to find the place. A songfest began before dark and in a few minutes people began to gather by the hundreds. They walked from their own village some of which was as much as twenty miles away. Now days a block is too far to go to church on foot but it didn't deter them. As sundown began to approach the men began to sing and praise the Lord and soon the film 'Jesus' was shown. Following that showing an invitation was given and several hundred came forward to learn more about Jesus. That was just the beginning of the surprise for me. A Bible study was held the next morning and again the Jesus film was shown that evening and during the two evenings over 500 people made professions of faith in God. Sunday morning the Bible study was held and then the worship service with over 1000 people present and soon a new church was formed with 120 members. If that can be done in Africa why can't it be done in America? I wish I had the memory and ability to put everything that we experienced there in this book but I'm sure I would leave out the best so I try to get the things that really thrilled me as I saw what the Holy Spirit can do with dedicated people.

We did take a bit of vacation at the suggestion of the missionaries and drove north to the Kasungu national park. It was a game park where the animals wandered about without worry and were kept in the area by keeping a lake full of water from which they didn't wander. The lions were not often visible but were there and elephants were very visible. Water buffalo, deer and elk were easy to find and hippos could be found in or near the lake. It was an interesting place to visit and we stayed longer than we should because gas stations all closed at five and we were low on gas and the closest station was half an hour away and we deep in the park. On the way out a new thing met us, not an animal but a fire that raged high in the air. The park rangers burn away the underbrush regularly so new grass will grow so we were to observe their fire. The problem was it was on both sides of the road we were traveling and Georgia did not like that. I knew we would not make it to a gas station but I was determined to get out of the park and hope one was still open. As we went past the fire we could feel the heat coming in the windows but it was far enough away that it could not do any damage. Georgia again doubted my sanity. As we left the park the gas gage was already touching the empty mark, No stations open and we had over 90 miles to go. That reminded me of "coming in on a wing and a prayer" and I new it was time to ask God for help. I drove very cautiously and took advantage of each hill and shut the engine off to coast down the hill. We made it and the next morning I got to the station and the car died just as I pulled in the driveway. God answers prayer.

We had the opportunity to visit Zomba plateau south of Lilongwe and that was a beautiful trip. I'm not sure how high Zomba Mountain was but you could see for miles from a lodge on the top. There were lakes, trails and cabins there but we were not planning to spend the night. I had taken my fishing rod and a few lures and caught fish in one of the lakes. Guards were posted in all kinds of places in Malawi and I don't know why but the guard here looked hungry so I offered him the three fish. He didn't want to take it because I had caught it and it was mine to keep. I told him I had no way to cook it so he accepted and I'm sure enjoyed it. Again we had to call on the Lord because our gas tank was down to ¼ tank and we had over a hundred miles to go to get home again. It was past 5 and stations were closed until eight the next morning. My instinct told me it was not wise to sit along the road but we left and by driving careful and letting the car coast down the hills we managed to make it to within two miles from home. We were near the publishing house so I walked there to use the phone and got Jerry to bring me a little gas from the garage. God is so good to us.

The first year we were in Malawi was very inspirational for us and we will never forget many good friends we met there and fellowshipped with. As we witnessed so many people with so little, we were reminded of the 30s when people took care of each other. When a farmer was sick or injured the neighbors all helped them to keep the work done. We relied on each other for survival and every one was so happy and joyful and life was so simple. People in Malawi were very courteous and helpful and went out of the way to help us. On one occasion we were traveling to Mzuzu to visit the Swaffords and on the way visited the village of our yardboy. We were told we were the first white people to visit their village and they were thrilled to feed us a bowl of rice. Had we made an appointment they would have fed us a 'feast of a beast' probably a chicken. The yard boy interpreted for us and later drew a map so we would not get lost getting back to the road. We didn't read right or the map was not right and we did get lost.

After driving miles out of the way and not finding the 'highway' we finally stopped and picked up a hitchhiker. Georgia was sure that was a mistake but he eventually led the right way and we came to the tarmac road very near his home. I stopped and thanked him and told him I could now find my way but he insisted on going on with us to Mzuzu to make sure we made it. It was already dark and I didn't want him to walk back to Equandeni but he insisted and got out of the car to walk 15 miles back to his home. Another angel had attended us and we thanked the Lord for this mans' concern and help. It would be impossible to relate all the times we enjoyed their hospitality and care.

Visiting a church was a great experience. As we arrived we were greeted with a muli brengi and we replied ndili bwino. That greeting had to be repeated with each one even though they were all right there together. 'you are how' 'we are good' were things we heard each time we met someone and it became a habit very soon and seemed to thrill them that we could use that much of their language.

The choir at Lilongwe Baptist was made up of 5 to 70 year olds and the 5s sang out with great voice and were a great part of the joy of our stay there. Our last Sunday there I was asked to speak and the choir was very special that day. We had just received word that my father had passed away and as if by a miracle we were able to get a plane home just in time to reach the church for the funeral. That was a sad day and yet a grand day. Dad had lived near 90 years for the Lord and was now in His hands and we were back to see family. Dads' funeral was held in Savannah, Mo. And Rev. Doyle Sager officiated and delivered a very evangelistic sermon. Before the message he asked the congregation how many had been won to Christ under Bro. Billies ministry. Almost every hand went up and the church was filled to capacity. He then asked how many pastors were there that had begun their ministry under Bro. Billie. There were nearly 50 hands went up to show the effects of what God can to do with one who is willing to fully surrender. It was very sad leaving the people we had learned to love and did not expect to see them again. That would change though in 1978 as we were privileged to return.

Phase XI
Home again

In the next few years I worked for MNEA again and Mom worked for Scholastics and we kept busy at church. The kids were scattered about the country but were always a short distance away and able to see us. The call to return was exciting but we didn't know how our kids would react to leaving again. It didn't take long till they were encouraging us and we began to make arrangements. The first time we let the kids used the house but they were not available this time so we found a renter. That turned out to be a mistake but at least we felt free to leave.

We received tickets in a short time and were driven to the airport with 'all our' luggage again. It wasn't as difficult getting on a plane then as it is now but waiting is always an expected thing. This trip was not as new to us now and we were on a different plane and route. This time we landed in London but could not do much but peek out the window but we didn't wait long and were on the next plane that took us to Addis Abba and on to Lilongwe. We were joined, on that flight, by a family going to Zimbabwe, and the father was a dentist and missionary. The children entertained us.

Phase XII
Back where we belong

As usual, we were met, by Missionaries and Malawians and it was a joyous reunion. Things had changed a lot by then with new buildings, new people and a new pastor. Rev. Malikano would be our new pastor and he was there to meet us.

Some space had been added to the plant and several staff members had changed but it was still in working order. Other changes had taken place that bothered me a lot. All supplies were now locked up and I was told that someone was still steeling things. After getting acquainted with the new people there and in the community an Indian printer called me to tell me one of my employees was selling some things he was sure came out of our supplies. I went to check and certainly those supplies were ours and the one selling them to him was a new employ that somehow managed to sneak them out. He was confronted and fired but not sent to jail as was expected. In Malawi and maybe some other countries when a person was accused he went to jail until someone felt sorrow for him and got a lawyer to get him out. That could take weeks.

Some new equipment was purchased and Jerry Dowdy went to South Africa to get it. A truck had been purchased to haul maize to feed those that had none to eat. Jerry drove to South Africa to purchase supplies and came back with a truck loaded with 'stuff' for the press and the mission. It takes three days to make that trip which includes clearing three boarders. Each one can take hours to get through but the clearing of the load takes a lot of time. I would like to relate every occasion of our fellowship times with the missionaries. We would get together to play games, eat and sometimes just fellowship but it was great times.

Georgia often walked to the store to buy groceries and it was a short distance. One corner had a path that cut across the lot and saved some time but it was shocking for her one time when she felt something touch her bag and looked down just in time to see a man grab her purse out of the bag. That included her passport and drivers license and that was critical. The purse was found near by and only the money was missing so she did not have to go through the ordeal of getting a new passport.

As seniors we did not have to take a test to get the license but the paper work and standing in line was enough.

I must say more about the beauty of the country because it was really a sight to behold. The seasons are reverse of ours since Malawi was 15 degrees south of the equator and we are north. We arrived at the beginning of the rainy season and the Jakaronda trees were full of purple blooms. The Poinsetia bushes, which were over six feet tall were in full bloom. Flamboyent trees that lined the streets were covered with brilliant red blooms to highlight the street. The one I tested in Blantyre but cannot remember the name of not only beautiful but very aromatic. I do expect heaven to be <u>much </u>more so but that was impressive. The Lilongwe River ran through the middle of the old town and was a pretty river in normal times. It did flood during the rainy season and could be very destructive. It was also the laundry room for many nationals as well as a place to bath. There was grave danger though that made people very alert. Crocodiles lived in the river and were always ready for a meal. Those bathing or doing their laundry learned to leave as others did because crocs waited till most were gone to attack. Those crocs were very large.

Mary Anne Chandler was a single Woman Missionary. She worked with women to teach them to raise their families right and healthy. She lived in a nice house and had a housekeeper and yard boy that was very nice. He had a wife and five children, I think. His wife died and Mary Anne took care of his children as though they were her own. She loved them and taught them a lot including English. The yard boy also died and Mary Anne adopted the children and brought them to America when she came home on furlough. It was sad to hear she developed cancer and died before returning to Malawi. I have wondered what happened to the children.

The Garners were the agricultural missionaries and lived on the farm near Balaka and their mission was to teach the Malawians better ways to farm. Van and Mary Thompson had raised two boys there while working in various capacities with the nationals. Barbara and Gene Kingsley, the tallest of them, that stood out among the Malawians. So many people and places that were so impressive to us and I wish I could remember them all.

Marlyn and Sam Upton were of special interest to us because they were from Missouri and they had a very cute little girl that was full of energy. She played with the Malawian children and was a real standout since she was very pale in color and the children there were very black.

The Workmans, had two children and they were very sweet and helpful. Debby the daughter loved horses and an Indian painter came to town and she got him to paint horses all over her room.

It is hard to believe those little children are now married and have children of their own and some are in missionary work themselves. May God give them a very happy life.

There were so many interesting things about the visit there and I know I will leave out some very good parts. Like watching the women mold and bake the pottery, molding the mud bricks for the homes, carving objects in wood and ivory and even stone. To watch men row the boats, carved out of baobab trees and dragging them out to go fishing. Even their fishing methods were interesting. Two men would drag the net out with the boat with one end tied to the bank. The net would be several hundred feet long and have long ropes on each end with the one end tied down and spread it in a large circle to be lowered down as they pulled it along. The other end would be pulled back to the bank so several men could start to pull it in.

As they pulled it in very rhythmically they sang a chorus I don't remember. It reminded me of the old 'gandy dancers' that laid down the railroad and sang as they went. As the men on the bank pulled the net in one of the men in the boat was in the water to make sure the net didn't get caught on something on the bottom. He had to watch for hippos as well to warn them of a danger because the hippo would tear up the net and maybe drag them in. As they pulled the net in several people would be ready to grab the fish and put them in buckets or bags. The smallest to the largest were saved and the smallest were laid on rocks to be sun dried. Very tiny ones called 'usipa' dried very fast and were eaten then for renewing their strength. Just drop them in your mouth whole. I tried some and they were all right after you got them past your nose. As you might expect the dry fish was very smelly but cooked with the seasoning they used they made a tasty treat. Watching the monkeys and baboons running around to grab the fish or anything eatable was like watching a circus and it took a lot of help to run them off.

Several cultural things faced us and we had to abide by them or be embarrassed. You always shake hands with the right hand but with the left hand gripping the wrist of the right. This was to indicate that you did not have a knife or club behind your back. A carry over from the days of tribalism I guess. You never offer anyone anything with the left hand or they would refuse it. The left hand was used for wiping and not always sterile. Many words we commonly used were used in a different way or had a different meaning. Cars were 'galimotos', hoods were 'bonnets', and trunks were 'boots'. I was sure glad they were jovial about our mistakes.

The open markets provided food of all kinds for us and it was interesting to go there. There was always plenty of vegetables and fruit as well as meat. The meat could be beef (hanging in the hot kiosk) or chicken. Occasionally there would be goat, mice or any beast. The fish market was strong smelling but very safe in the morning. Food was not all that was available. There were tools, car parts, and appliance parts or about any thing you needed. I also found some tools there that were missing from the mission compound. We purchased a reed basket that was perfect for a laundry basket and it is still as good as new today. Artists of all kinds displayed their work in the market but they preferred to do so, on parking lots where they didn't pay for the space. One artist was born without arms and painted with his feet. An amazing fellow and very friendly. We bought several of his paintings.

Near the end of our stay in Malawi, Don McNeely in Zambia contacted us about going there to assist in the publishing house. That sounded like an interesting challenge but we had not made arrangements to do so and a return home would be necessary. We didn't know what our kids would think but knew if it was the Lords will the arrangements could be made. The return home was great and our growing family showed us a lot of love but did not object to our going to Zambia. We spent three months at home and made arrangements for the sale of our house. The deal was closed the day we were to take off.

Phase XIII
Zambia

The flight was normal and as boring as the other trips we had made but on a different route. We landed in daylight and could see what the world was like but it was not much different than Malawi. One noticeable difference was the town and because we arrived on the better side of town. The airport was several miles out of town and what we could see on the road was not much like what we had seen before. When we got closer to town the buildings seemed more modern and the mud brick huts were not visible. Lusaka is a large city and covers a lot of territory. The homes and businesses are almost all surrounded by large walls. This indicated to me that crime was prevalent and that meant this might not be as pleasant a visit. Once we arrived at the mission compound and met the missionaries we were greeted with a great welcome and quickly felt at home. We were to occupy the apartment normally used by the Hubbards who were on stateside assignment and it was very nice. The Allens lived in the apartment above and a single missionary, Janie House, lived upstairs on the other end. Later the Barbours would move in to the one across from us. They were all very nice to fellowship with and when we had free time would get together and play table games or work puzzles. Joe and Carol Barbour were Missourians and Carols sister and husband operated the More4less store in Jeff City. I was soon introduced to the publishing house and staff and thankfully the same language was in use. At least I could greet them in their own tongue. The equipment in the press had many needs and the personnel had a lot to learn. The dark room was in pretty good shape but the camera man had little experience and was not getting very good negatives so I had to correct that to start so we had better negatives to work with. The press, folder and the assembly space needed improvement but the major problem for me was the system. After visiting the government plant I realized the problem and it took some doing to make changes. The practice there and in Malawi was alike in that they followed a British means of keeping things straight. When a printing job was started nothing else was started until that one was finished. That meant only one person or crew was working while the others waited. What a waste of personnel and time. It took some time to get them to realize they could all be busy on their work and more could get done. The plant published 60 different books or tracts that year to exceed by 40 the amount finished the year before.

As in Malawi the manager of any business was responsible for employees at the time of a family members death. As a result I supplied a 'box' and transportation to the funeral and cemetery, usually acted as the hearse and what ever else was needed. Funerals were different there as you might expect and I was in the dark about it. In Malawi I attended several funerals and that only involved attending because they were all held in the village. Here in Zambia they were all in this large city that I didn't know very well. The first one I was involved with was that of the father of one of the staff. He lived out at the edge of town and I had gone to his home to pick him up and take him to the hospital because he had a bad case of pneumonia. It was during the rainy season and I had to drive through a 'chug' hole three feet deep to get to his house. The next day he died and I had to go with the pickup I was driving and pick the body up at the morgue and take it to the home for preparation for the funeral. Embalming was seldom used and the funeral had to be held soon. The family always gathered around the home and the women sat around the 'box' while someone cooked nsima for all the guests. As you might expect the guest list would grow as the neighbors learned there was a funeral so there might be 500 people to get a meal. No one objected as they knew they would all do the same if the meal was free. As everyone had eaten, the body was loaded on the pickup and all the people that could hold on climbed on top of the 'box' or where ever they could hold on, at least fifteen on this occasion. I drove to the cemetery and the body was placed on a table and opened for people to observe and then carried to the burial plot some 100 yards away. As I watched I was amazed at the number of graves that were opened and ready for a burial. Some times there were as many as fifty burials per day in one cemetery. With the AIDs problem I imagine it is worse now.

The Zambia Baptist Seminary was adjacent to this cemetery and was a nice school and grounds and well kept like a park, a pretty place to see.

The publishing house here had a kitchen and a place for the employees to eat. The cooks were good and offered food to me but I usually went home for dinner and to rest a bit. Home wasn't very far and I was sure I would have no problem finding it that first day. I failed to make one turn and ended up lost and had to drive back and start over. I did make it the second time and Georgia had gone to the market with Joy Allen. No food after all. Larry Dramon was the finance director or something and his wife Jonda was in South Africa expecting a baby. A new little boy was added to the mission. Before we left we were invited to his birthday party and watched as he stuck his face in the cake to eat it. We acted as house sitters for the Dramons while they were on holiday.

Fred Allen found out I worked on appliances so an additional task came to fill my time. I failed to mention that both in Malawi and Zambia time is flexible. A meeting might be set for two o'clock but might not start till three. However the workers were expected to be at work on time and usually were. They cherished their jobs.

We were members of the Woodland Baptist Church, which was some distance away from where we lived, but was a very friendly fellowship and most of the members spoke English. The service was in Chichewa but we enjoyed the people and the fellowship. The church had a floor of large stones of different colors that were just laid on the ground that had been well leveled. As time went by termites decided to build a nest below the church. Soon after we began to attend there I notice fine sawdust below the back pew and on inspection found the termites had found a hole through the rocks and gone into the pew to devour the wood. We replaced the bad wood and poured creosote in the ant hole and filled it up. That probably will not stop them from coming in again but will help for a few years. Termites were a problem in Zambia and Malawi and not only built large mounds above the ground but left a large hole in the ground where the mound came from. Those large holes were often used as chimbudsi or outdoor toilets. Just a bamboo wall on three sides and it was ready.

They didn't seem to bother that the termites were destructive because they became a delicacy when the rains started and vigorously caught them as they flew out of the holes by the hundreds.

Donna Collier was another volunteer and a joy to be around. She was jovial but serious about her work. We were invited to accompany her and the Allens on a trip to Zimbabwe to visit a game park and that became a real adventure. Donna had borrowed a video camera from Joe Barbour to take pictures of the trip but wouldn't let me touch it because it was borrowed. When we were about through the trip she discovered the tape had the tab out of it and she had no pictures. That was a shame for it was a very interesting trip with a variety of exciting happenings.

We had gone to the wrong gate to get in and were told to drive 100 miles further to the other gate. When we were ready to leave a tire on the car was flat and another couple stopped to see if we needed help. We learned they were from northwest Missouri and had known the Heriford preachers, including my father. While on that tip we visited Victoria Falls that lies just inside Zimbabwe. We stayed in cabins along the Zambezi River and watched animals along the river. We went on a walking safari with an armed guard and saw a herd of impala, rhinos, giraffes, baboons and elands. Later we took a bus tour of about ten miles and saw many animals and birds typical of only Africa. A cheetah had caught a dakur (a small deer) and was being interrupted by vultures. One ostrich was off in the distance. As we were leaving Zimbabwe we stopped at a large hotel to find a bite to eat (Livingstone Hotel) and ate in an open courtyard and watched musicians playing on home made marimbas that were from two feet long to eight feet long. They sounded great but I was out of film and didn't get a picture.

We were invited to a small village church, several miles west of Lusaka, by a seminary student, mainly because he needed a ride home, but also to see a gold mine. The gold mine was one the government had sold to an individual because it failed to produce enough to be profitable. A man of Indian descent owned it and was glad to show us the grinding equipment and gold ore. As I watched the process I thought of the many times gold is shown in movies as a shiny bit of gold as it is picked from the river bottom. What a joke since gold has to be smelted before it looks gold. The owner offered me a large chunk of gold ore but I broke off a small piece to keep. We visited that small church and sat on pews made of mud bricks and watched the preacher standing behind a pulpit made of mud bricks.

Work at the publishing house was interrupted by a fire caused by a faulty fan. It started just after we closed and one person was still there to notice it and call the fire department. Extensive damage was caused in the pressroom and the ceiling and roof burned away leaving it open to the rains. We had several boxes of Bibles stored in that room and most were damaged. The next day several firemen came and asked if they could have one of the damaged Bibles and I was surprised because they were all Muslim. A number of books were on tables in that room waiting to be finished and most were heavily damaged or destroyed. Contractors were called in and the work got underway but we lost a lot of time as a result of the fire.

Missionaries gather for planning meetings on a regular basis and eat and fellowship, like one big happy family. It is a time for all of them in each area to plan for future needs and programs. One night I had a dream that we were all in such a meeting and my father came to me looking like a young man. He had passed away several months before and he was in his late 80s then. His visit was very brief as he touched my shoulder to get my attention and said Jay I just came for her. Everything seemed so normal about it but I knew my mother had passed away. The next morning my brother back in the states called to tell me about her death and I told him I already knew about it as Dad had come to tell me. He was so overcome with emotion that he couldn't talk but I assured him I was fine.

We were not able to get home for mothers funeral, as flights out of Zambia were not easy to arrange. We completed our assignment in Zambia and felt we had experienced some wonderful things. The beauty of Gods Africa, the beauty of the people and the beauty of Gods working through His Holy Spirit and the many dedicated missionaries. We had truly been blessed by the power of Gods Love.

More about our visit to Africa can be found in the book "Africa? What are we doing here"

Phase XIV
At Home Again

We left Zambia on Zambia Airlines and landed in New York at one airport and had to fly to the other airport by a rickety sounding helicopter to catch a TWA plane to St. Louis and transfer to a smaller airline to get to Jefferson City. We left Zambia and 90 degree weather and landed in JC where it was near 20 degrees. It was like an instant freeze and we were not dressed for cold weather. The whole family was there to meet us, and a few extras. The following two weeks we spent in one room at Gladys' house as we proceeded to buy the little house next to her. Sixteen years we have been here and after a little repair and remodeling it became a nice comfortable home. To some this house would seem pretty lowly but we felt wealthy after seeing people living in a one-room hut with a dirt floor and it was only the size of our living room. As I look back I wish I could share my wealth with them as they shared their hospitality with us.

The furnace in the new house was an old floor furnace and very rusty. There was no basement so sons, grandsons and neighbors helped to dig out a 12x12 space and pour concrete floor so I could install a forced air furnace and remove the old rusty one that leaked fumes. Vinyl siding was added to improve the looks and avoid painting the old wood siding and a little paint on the trim and we were very happy with our retirement home with 50x400 foot lot and garden space. A few years later the back room, that had been a porch but enclosed to make a room, began to leak so I took it off and after a lot of dirty work added a larger room that is more useful and has a good roof. I have a number of friends and family to thank for its completion. Completion was a rush necessity since it included the bathroom and a bathroom in USA is for some reason a necessity.

Many interesting things have happened in the last 25 years that I wish I could tell moment by moment but who would want to listen to 25 years of stories except my grand kids and they wouldn't listen very long? I have enjoyed fishing some and it is always nice to have a son along but Herb thinks that might be bad. On one occasion Herb and I went to Mark Twain Lake to try it out. It was a nice day though a little breezy but tempting none the less and we put the boat in the water. The other side always looks better so we headed there with great hopes. As we approached the other side I felt the need to turn around to face the other end of the boat. That would have made it easier to fish. However I lost my balance and fell backwards over the side with my legs still in the boat. That made it easy for the boat to roll over and spill every thing in the water. It so happened that the water was shallow enough that we could get our feet to the ground and rapidly try to salvage all our important equipment. We managed to set every thing on the bank and drag the boat to the edge where we could tip it over and drain it. The breeze was quiet cool with our clothes wet but it also was handy for drying them. After an hour of fishing there we crossed to the other side to try and ended up getting wet again as the waves beat against the front of the boat and splashed the water in our face. That was not our best fishing trip but it was memorable.

We renewed our relationship with Calvary Baptist Church that had been praying for us the entire time we were gone. We had been associated with Calvary from the day we moved to Jefferson City and had been very involved in every part of it. In 1981 when we went to Malawi Al Ewens was recording the services and sending us a tape so we could keep up with the work back home. We missed the people in Malawi but it was nice to be home with friends we had known and loved for years. We had the privilege of going to other churches to tell them of our journey and remind them that they could also have that joy by volunteering to help with whatever talent the Lord had given them. Several years before a group from Calvary had gone on a short-term mission trip to Blackhat, New Mexico to rebuild a campground and hold VBS for Navajo children. That was a real joy and inspired us to make other such trips, one to Pelston, Michigan and another to Blackwell, Oklahoma. God has blessings waiting for us if we are ready for them. We were not trained for what we did but God made the difference.

God made a difference in our lives and I hope a difference in other lives as well. Our return to Calvary Baptist Church was a real joy and we were ready to get back to work at home but it was disappointing to find the church was not doing as well as the churches in Africa. We wanted to see churches and people grow and reach out to others but there seemed to be little progress in that direction. Pastors did not seem to be enthused about the needs of people in the community as those in Malawi. The major excitement here seemed to be settling disputes. Our hearts desire was that people here were as loving and caring as those we had worked with in Africa.

Rev. C. D. Butler was serving as interim pastor at Liberty Road Baptist Church in Taos, Mo. and little progress was being made there so Georgia and I felt the Lord might want us to go there to encourage C. D. and the church to reach out to the community and minister to them. It was during this time I had an urge (or call of God) to write a paper about what I felt was a serious problem in our churches today. 'The failure of Christians to really care.' I plan to include that at the end of this book with hopes that it will inspire pastors and others to look seriously at how we are carrying out the command of Christ.

As usual the work at Liberty Road was slow because the big interest was settling miss-understanding. Following Rev. Butlers' resigning a young businessman came to fill the pulpit until a new pastor could be found. He was not an ordained minister but he had a heart to be one and he was much appreciated. We did get him to come as interim for a while and he was an inspiration to all and we tried to get him to come as full time but he felt his business kept him too busy to do a good job as full time pastor. After some searching a pastor was called and he seemed to be enthusiastic but was also very proud of being the pastor. His actions caused great distress between members and an unwise business meeting caused several to leave. He resigned after that and the church is again hoping to find a pastor who is ambitious for the Lord.

Georgia and I had always had good health and although we had colds and the like we were generally healthy. She had an ovarian tumor removed while expecting Gladys and I some trouble with pneumonia. In 1995 I began to have some trouble with my legs, which called for tests to find the cause. In the testing process a doctor decided I needed my carotid artery cleaned out and I was reluctant, but it was accomplished. I later had a large hernia repaired. God had been good to us and gave us good health for what He wanted us to do. Doctor James Allen was our family doctor for many years and I appreciate him very much.

It was during the years that Bro. Dale was pastor there that Georgia was diagnosed with incurable lymphoma. That came as shock to the church and to the family but she continued participation at church and maintained a great hope in the Lord knowing that she was ready to go to be with Him. For three years she went through treatments that seemed to make things worse but she struggled with it until March 22, 2005. She was always faithful to church and family.

After Georgia's death I began to go to Calvary since it was close by but I continued to be concerned about Liberty

Road because an evangelical church is badly needed in the Taos area. I have been thrilled at the love and concern of the members at Calvary and the way things have grown. I have joined the choir even though I am too old to be much at singing but I do enjoy it. My daughter Rose had provided me with a tape recorder to record our experiences in Africa but I chose to put it on computer where I could edit it.

Ralph Farris died February 24, 2001 and his funeral was very unusual in that he provided the music for his funeral. He was an accomplished musician able to play most any instrument and had recorded several pieces he had played on the organ. Those tapes were the music for his funeral.

I am enjoying being at home although alone but not totally. My son Dick, son Mark stop by to visit and keep me company and Herb still calls for help on his presses and goes fishing with me occasionally. Granddaughter Heather and her four drop in regularly to check on me and visit when there is time in their schedule and often come over to watch a TV show. I am grateful for the company and enjoy the fellowship at church so I am not alone. God is always here.

As time went by our children went their way and found their own lives to raise their own families. It has been a delight to have them drop in to visit or to send me emails. Gladys moved to Arkansas with her family, Richard Tiffany her husband and two sweet teenagers, Kalila and Ezra. Dick remains in Jefferson City with his family of two boys and one girl and a very nice wife, Marcia. We are grateful for her taking care of Dick while home schooling a granddaughter. Jason and Dusten are the sons and Lacey the daughter and between them they have four beautiful daughters. Herb is still in Jefferson City and operates his own printing plant. He and Cheri have one daughter, Sara and one son Joshua. Mark still lives In

Jefferson City and stops by to check on me regularly while taking care of his wife Barbara. Rose also left town and went all the way to Florida with her husband Richard and three boys, Michael, Aaron and Tyler. Richard is busy with his brothers in construction business there but they manage to come visit at least twice a year. Richard and Aaron were involved in a serious accident last year and thank God he is now back to work. It is always great to have them visit but I think of them often and know they are near in my heart.

As I look back over these 82 years little bits of stories pop into my mind. The time Georgias brother and I were fishing on the MariDesiegn river and a pair of coons shocked us with a loud howl on a very quiet night. The times we managed to enter the wrong highway go north instead of south. The trip to Pikes Peak on July third and run into a snow storm and two motorcycles coming down the mountain looking around the windshield to see to drive. The time the Honda timing belt broke and I change it along side the highway. Many more I could relate if you want to come by and set awhile.

I'm sure this leaves a lot of our lives unknown but at 81 I am afraid time is too short to elaborate.

This writing is not just about Georgia and I, but about a family headed by Audra and Billie Heriford from which it originated. Bro. Billie was a pastor that knew what the Bible taught and he tried to share with his part of the world, the message that "God is Love" to everyone the world over. His power is available to all who will ask for and accept it. God, through Jesus, gave those who claimed His promise the order to go to the needy and share with them all that they had been blessed with including the message that God loved them. As I have watched so many churches begin to dwindle in attendance and spirit and seen the growth of churches in Africa I felt compelled to put into words, the things I am sure my father would preach if he were still alive. Those words are a great concern to me and I hope will some day be a concern to pastors the world over.

I have heard many people say God had not given them any special talents so they couldn't do much. I have also seen people that had no talent but accepted God's challenge and accomplished great things. My father was one of those people and I think he was very successful and loved what God gave him to do. I think God gave me several talents and I probably overlook most of them. He gave me the privilege of flying and I enjoyed that. He also gave me opportunities to do other things to minister to people. I mentioned earlier a little about working on cars. I had no training for that but I had read in Paul's letters that we can do all things through Christ who strengthens us and I claimed that promise each time I received a challenge that I felt was an opportunity to help someone.

A doctor friend had several antique cars and few mechanics want to work on them. Most of them many people have never heard about. One was 1937 Cord with a number of conveniences that did not show on cars till the 50s. One was a 1921 Duesenberg that would be very expensive. I had never seen either of these but I knew if I asked God for advice He would be ready to help. In other words, I believe in prayer not just for our health, I believe God will give us what we need. All we have to do is be in an attitude of prayer 24 hours a day, not just fifteen minutes every morning.

Another surprising thing occurred soon after Georgia's death that seemed like an answer to prayer. My sister called for a visit by phone and during the conversation informed me that my first girl friend, Pauline Hollis, of years ago had lost her husband by a serious illness about the time Georgia passed away. I had not seen her or heard from her in years but felt like sending her a sympathy card. In a few days I received a short letter from her that has become a means of passing the long days. We have been in constant contact since and renewed our relationship of 1944. It has been a joy to say the least since Georgia is gone. We have exchanged information and shared concerns as though we have really renewed old acquaintances and if we never have the chance to meet again it has been a joy to be reminded that we were young once. Pauline was not the typical only child but very quiet and humble. I really liked her but God had other plans for both of us and I'm sure God's plan was best.

THE BALL BEGAN TO ROLL

A discussion of the slow growth of evangelical churches in America and abroad.

Why are the churches losing ground and not growing?

SNOWBALLS WILL ROLL

The winter of 2005 was not a seriously bad winter weather wise but there was one good snow early in the winter that brought joy to one little boy who lives in Florida. He used to live in Missouri but it was a few years ago and he had not seen snow since he left. He was not a happy boy for a few days but when the snow arrived he was quick to run out to play in his short pants and little else.

The big event is always to build a snowman and the work began before breakfast. The first ball was rolled around for quite a while until it was sufficient for the body, then an upper body and finally the head. There is something about rolling a ball of snow that you are tempted to keep rolling and rolling to see how big you can make it.

That seems to be the way life is. When something is attractive we want more of it whether or not we need it or whether or not it is wise.

I once saw a video of a snowball turned loose on a hill and it grew larger and larger until it crashed into a home and destroyed it. That is what sin can do and is doing continually.

That is the basis of these thoughts.

The Wandering Israelites

In the early years of the Israelites, after they had entered the Promised Land, God had provided protection for them from their enemies. He had promised to provide all their needs and to make them a great nation. They lived well and God blessed them with large families and a wealth of goods. The only requirement for their success was to obey their God and worship Him only. When they first took the land they were told to destroy any sign of idolatry, including those who worshipped those idols. It went well for a few years until some began to marry into the families of the idol worshipers. Of course it seemed all right for those individuals to bring their "Gods" with them as long as the Israelites weren't involved. Then it seemed a simple thing and surely couldn't hurt to watch. Then the ball began to roll.

As you read the story of these people you realize they didn't intend to drift into idolatry it just happened. In the book of the judges you find the sentence repeated after each judge dies "and there rose up a nation that knew not God". God still had mercy on His people and sent another judge to save them from their enemies and turn them back to the one who brought them out of bondage and into the Promised Land. No, they had not planned it that way they just let it happen because they had forgotten their promise to God.

The Books of Kings and Chronicles repeats those stories and tells of various kings who themselves were easily led into idolatry because they didn't follow the instructions God had given them. When God gave Moses the law He instructed them to teach their children the story of how God had led them out of Egyptian bondage and into the Promised Land. How He had fed them when there was no food available, provided water in a desert land, and fought for them when they were outnumbered. They were just like people today and said to themselves "they will hear about it sometime, somewhere". Doesn't that sound just like our time?

And the ball continued to roll.

THE WANDERING AMERICANS

When the Church in England began to be the ruler of all and set its own rules of conduct and worship, the same thing began to happen to them. Things became so difficult that people could not really worship God but only the "Church". When Godly people began to feel uncomfortable about the way they were to worship they decided to leave for a place of peace and a place to worship the way they felt God intended. God blessed them in doing so and with His help they made a dangerous journey across a dangerous sea to find that new life.

The pilgrims worked hard with their hands to start a new life with freedom of worship and freedom of speech. Many died before being able to fully enjoy that new freedom but they had a big part in a new beginning. It took many months of enduring the cold, the shortage of food and the loss of many things they enjoyed in the old country. With hard work and the cooperation of some Native Americans their labors paid off. Gardens began to supply good food and houses were built to make the cold winters livable and the rains and snows acceptable. As time went on the people began to form an organization that was to foster more cooperation and provide a form of stability to their lives. This new government was a blessing to their existence.

As humans go they were 'very human' and many developed strong feelings for a control over all worship so as to make sure it never developed into what they experienced in the homeland. Now that sounds like a good idea but who is to determine the proper way to worship? There were some that wanted quiet worship experience. Some wanted exuberant worship experiences. Of course there were other ideas that entered into the picture and soon the lack of Christ-like love turned the whole colony into a "witch-hunt" situation that brought disaster to the great plan for freedom of worship.

Eventually a government was formed that was based on the teachings in the Bible. A constitution was written with all the right freedoms that would guarantee freedom for all to worship as they chose without fear of either the church or the government interfering. This government was to be governed by the people and for the people.

As time passed it seems some citizens decided the people were not smart enough to make decisions and took it upon themselves to misinterpret the constitution to make it fit their agenda and not the public. Since many citizens were not concerned a new attitude developed that has caused us to continue to drift farther and farther from a Christian nation for which it was formed. That attitude of 'so what' has opened the door for non-Christian groups to gain control of our lives whether we like it or not.

The prophets warned the children of Isreal of impending doom if they did not change. Jeramiah warned them but they did not listen and he saw that destruction take place.

There is an attitude that encompasses tolerance and acceptance that has caused many to accept what ever challenges our faith and we don't seem to be concerned because 'everybody accepts' it. Thinking it will only affect a few people we pass it off as a natural trend. Such was the case with the Isrealites in Judea.

The ball kept rolling till it got to the bottom.

THE WANDERING CHURCHES

A long time ago God sent His Son to die on the cross for a very needy people. His Son suffered humiliation, pain and suffering but not before He went to the needy, the poor, the sick and the sinner. He went to them with a message of hope and joy. It was a message of relief from sorrow, grief, pain and guilt. A message of a God of Love, Love that could forgive the whole world of their sin and evil and take away the guilt. A message of a new life filled with Joy, Faith and Love. Love to share with others, faith to know and accept that God is always in control, Joy to praise God for who He is and what He has done and is doing.

So many churches try to do first what Jesus did last. Have a party or a banquet or a celebration to attract people and get them to come to join them in more of the same.

We plan training programs, hold Bible Studies; have learning experiences for all who will participate. Then invite them to come back for more of the same.

Christ did not teach His disciples to minister to 'target groups'. He didn't send them to Baptists, Methodists or Muslims. He sent them to everyone to take a glass of water to the thirsty, provide clothes to the needy, healing for the sick and especially hope and joy to the down trodden, joy that will open the door again while displaying the faith that God has put into their hearts. Without the joy strengthened by faith there is nothing that will attract mankind to the presence of God. Our purpose is to go to people and minister to them. If our lives are attractive because of our joy in the Lord and our desire to be like Him He will use our feeblest effort to open the hearts of the needy we try to minister to.

Eloquent speech and much practice in training sessions is not a requirement to do what Jesus did as He walked on this earth. In fact He sent out His disciples (untrained fishermen, tax collectors, all unlearned, plain men) and told them not to take extra clothes, food or even a planned script because he wanted the Holy Spirit to put words in their mouths and He knew their words would interfere. What greater preparation could you require?

Yes we need to know the words of our master. We need to study the Bible or we can't tell the story. How can we answer people's questions if we don't know the answers.

To some the answer to doing the Lord's work is having a large attractive building in which to perform. Jesus did not tell Peter to build a big beautiful church and form a nice choir. He said go to the highways and byways, the poor, the sick and those in prison and tell them of the wonders of God and the Love He bestows <u>and I will build the Church</u>.

Micah 6:8 says, "He has shown you O man, what is good; and what does the Lord require of you but to do justly, to love mercy and to walk humbly with your God. In other words "walk the talk". Or "put your money where your mouth is," You can't look at someone with a frown on your face and convince them that the Lord will bring happiness into their lives. Even a fake smile will not do the job. A sincere and humble "caring" is a necessity for sharing the Love of God to a nonbeliever or an uncertain one.

When people find the Lord, know the Bible and find the joy and freedom Christ brings, they are happy people rejoicing in the Lord always. They don't have to pretend to love others, it comes naturally. Even when life brings sorrow and difficulty they no longer depend on their own strength and abilities because the Holy Spirit is there to Help.

Afraid to knock on doors? .

Afraid to offer help to someone? Why?

Jesus said "do it and I'll be there to help"

There are some oft-repeated remarks that I find hard to accept.

1. Don't knock on some ones door unless you have made an appointment. How will they ever have the opportunity to hear?

2. Don't offer help to someone in need you could be sued.

3. Don't pick up hitchhikers they might kill you.

And Satan has many more but mainly "you might win someone to the Lord" so don't take a chance on danger.

When the Holy Spirit speaks wise people listen!

Danger is not a consideration. Responding to the Holy Spirit is.

What if it's the wrong spirit? 1 John 4:1 says "try the spirits whether they be of God".

There is a phrase the youth of today are using in learning to fight temptation that is the perfect answer to this "What would Jesus do"? If we think of the life of Jesus and how He reacted to things Satan tried to get Him to do it should help us decide the origin of the spirit.

1 John 4:4 says "you are of God little children and have overcome them, because He who is in you is greater than he that is in the world".

Phillipians 4:4 "rejoice in the Lord always" because he has made a way. He has opened the door and it's time for us to step in.

Why don't people come when we invite them or come back after visiting? If you were to go to a theater to see a play or a movie and the narrator described its scenes and said goodnight to you would you go back? Of course not. You went to see the action not a narrator. People want to see some action in the lives of Christians. They want to see that Spirit at work. Not just words. Not just song and dance but true Godly Love in action, a Love that begins with a caring visit at work, in their home or on the street.

THE WANDERING PREACHERS
Years ago young men felt there was a need to remind people of the story of the death and resurrection of Jesus Christ. Somehow the Holy Spirit warned them of the impending doom of the American people if they forgot that God had brought them to this "promised land". They didn't go to seminary to know how to warn the people, they just knew what the Bible taught and listened to the Holy Spirit.

Jesus told His followers to go in faith and the Spirit would tell them what to say and would provide all they needed.

They were not to take extra clothing, food or even a script (a special sermon) or even notes. He wanted the Holy Spirit to do the talking. It seems now that only a degree can talk. My Bible tells me that we who have put our trust in Jesus are all saints and therefore are in touch with that Spirit at all times.

The fact that we all have the ability to look to the Holy Spirit for wisdom at any time doesn't necessarily mean that we are all preachers but we can all be ministers. Giving a drink of water, a loaf of bread or offering assistance of any kind in Jesus' name is ministering. That is what we who are called Christians are to do.

So often pastors plan and organize programs and committees that take up vital time that should be spent walking the streets of the community and getting acquainted with the people we are to minister to. Some churches are so anxious to grow that they go clear across town to enlist people. If there is a special need for teachers or leaders that would be acceptable but our purpose as a church should be to minister to the people in the community around the church.

THE WANDERING CHRISTIANS

There is an attitude that encompasses tolerance and acceptance that has caused many to accept what ever challenges our faith and we don't seem to be concerned because 'everybody accepts' it. Thinking it will only affect a few people we pass it off as a natural trend. Such was the case with the Israelites in Judea.

It is true that the Bible doesn't teach total abstinence but it does teach responsibility, responsibility to our family, our friends and our neighbors. Paul told Timothy, and probably others, to drink a little wine for his stomachs sake. Some try to say the wine was not fermented but nature will tell you that it would be impossible to store it without it fermenting. Wine was often used because the water was not always safe. However Paul also told them not to be drunken with wine because they could not think clearly to carry out the work they were to be doing. It would also interfere with the influence they were to have on the people they tried to minister to.

Idols! What is an idol? They come in all sizes and shapes. Tall, thin, fat, round and square, wood, gold, copper, silver and some in flesh. Education might also be an idol if it becomes a priority.

Whatever stands in the way of our ministry becomes in some way an idol to us. A much cherished home, a nice car, a boat, or a bag of golf clubs. None of these are sinful in them selves but can be a hindrance to our accomplishing God's task. These are all things we as humans have and sometimes need but how do they fit into our priorities?

Many ideas sneak into our lives that seem to make sense but are not of the Holy Spirit. Just as the prophet Hananiah tried to console the children of Judah by telling them things were going to turn out just fine so 'no need to worry'. Our country is being bombarded with witchcraft for children in the games everyone else is playing. Some people who are considered to be smart insist there is a simpler way to be good without religion. Just meditate and study our inner-selves and we can achieve a better life. Maybe so but many people are going to meet Satan a lot sooner than they think. He is the author of such thinking and is a great promoter of it.

Where would we be if Jesus had chosen the easy way out? What would this world be like today?

Life has become so complicated that we have a hard time accomplishing the task we should complete. It is unheard of to turn the window crank in the car or unlock the door with a key. Adjusting the seat in the car must be done with a button. No wonder we as Americans are weak and over weight we do anything possible to avoid work. I have a cap that bears the words "who says nothing is impossible, I've been doing it for years" but is it easier to do less than the very best for our Lord? Why should we take shortcuts and the easy way out?

There is a song I haven't heard for some time but it is appropriate for this time. "Do we really care?" I often wonder whether we really have Gods' interests at heart or is it just a game? Is the Holy Spirit really a part of our lives or are we playing a game with Gods' promises?

We must remember that Gods' promises had a condition to them. Many people of generations past, including the Israelites, learned the hard way that God doesn't play games. He is very serious about His plan and His promises. He needs people to carry out His plan because He is not here on this earth to do it. By His Holy Spirit He gives power to achieve the impossible to those who are really concerned about the people in all parts of the world that have not heard about God's only Son that He allowed to die on the cross in our place. Do we really care or are we playing a game with religion as if it were a club to join?

Can we stop the ball before it's too late?

Only God knows the answer to that and it may be too late already. God may have given up on us like He did with the people of Sodom and Gomorrah.

What are we to do?

First we must get really serious about following God's plan and not ours. We must bow in total humility to His Spirit's leadership. Then we must listen closely to be sure we hear His voice and not our easy way out. Shortcuts may exist in God's plan but our shortcuts will surely fail.

There are many things that can be done to interest people in coming to our church. Musical programs, films or videos, there might even be a speaker worthy of attracting attention. But why do it at all unless we are really concerned about their lives and that it is the Spirit of God leading us to do it. God knows what we need to do and He will show us if we are ready. Ready--- to spend what He wants us to, ready to give the time required even if it means changing our worship time or giving an extra evening of personal time. Money should never be a deciding factor. Leaders should not be a factor. Only our faith and willingness is required.

Why us? Why our church? Because we are a part of the family of God and we are all responsible to those around us in regard to the joy they can have in a relationship to God.

I don't know it's origin but the phrase "if it's to be it's up to me" is very appropriate.

God made us all a little different, different in color, race, personality and even traits. He gave us each a different ability or talent and for a reason. He needed to reach different kinds of people and needed someone that was prepared for that purpose. As Paul said we are like different parts of the body put together to create a living being. Our legs do one thing our arms do another and our mouths do their job. Fully assembled the body does the work it was created to do.

The beginning of a growing church is putting the talents of its' members to work at what they know and enjoy. Putting them to work will require knowing what needs to be done in the community in which the church exists. It takes work to get members to state their abilities and to canvas the community to find ways to reach and to minister to people. This can be the real joy and blessing to members just to realize they are doing something that God can make use of. He will make use of it in His time and manner and we have no need to worry even though it seems nothing ever happens. As we visit homes we don't go there to convince people they are going to Hell but rather to let them see that there is peace and joy in being in the fellowship of a loving God. As we do as Jesus did and offer a loaf of bread or a drink of water we let the Holy Spirit take it from there. He knows the needs of the ones we try to minister to and He will fill those needs in His way and time. When we have a burden we are to take it to the Lord and leave it there. It is not our place to save people it is ours to have the joy of knowing that God will.

Heaven?
What will it be like?

Heaven has been described in many ways. A number of TV evangelists picture heaven as a beautiful place to behold. Streets of gold, jeweled mansions, ivory everywhere. What do you think it will be like?

Paul had an experience that gave a vague picture of what he saw. He didn't say it was jeweled, golden or silver. He just said it was indescribable. Other writers have written about the beauty of heaven and some have mentioned the streets of gold but would that be necessary?

Gold is the symbol of purity. Surely the streets of heaven will be pure, but gold? Paul talked about the crown of righteousness. Yes we can expect to wear a crown. Golden slippers? Certainly. Walking in pure steps. Heaven is not going to be what it is often pictured as, but it will be much more. As Paul said it will be indescribable.

Some talk of meeting long lost loved ones and what a joy that will be. To be back together again sounds great but is that what we can look forward to? A Pharisee came to Jesus with a tricky question that Jesus answered in His usual manner. The question was about the man whose brother had died and according to their tradition the next brother was required to take the brothers wife as his own. Other brothers died and the same tradition was required. Now he asked Jesus whose wife would be his in Heaven? Jesus answered with words that I think we should consider as an answer to our question. There will be no marriage or giving in marriage in Heaven. Who will we know and who will we look for when we get to heaven?

I am convinced that the only gold we will see in heaven will be the purity that will exist there. We will wear a crown of jewels as Paul mentioned but the jewels will be those who we influenced in life and became our brothers in heaven. We won't be looking down at those left behind since we would be looking at a sinful world and that would not be permitted in heaven. There will be no evidence of sin there. Only the glory of God and the Son sitting on the throne surrounded by the saints of all time. What greater heavenly thing could we seek?

Our sights on earth should be set on the goals Jesus set for us while He was on the earth. A drink of water (the water of Life) for the thirsty, a coat of care for the cold and homeless, a prayer of faith for those we are not able to serve personally. We should not be concerned about our rewards in heaven, they will mean very little to us when we see Jesus. What value could there be in a mansion or streets of gold? We will be too enthralled at the glory of all we see at the feet of our master.

The next question that comes to mind for me is when does heaven begin? Jesus said "bring your burdens to me and I will give you rest". Will we get to heaven or hell now? Many preachers and leaders preach about the promise of heaven and salvation from hell when Jesus said "I will give you rest". Why should we wait for the day we die and go to "heaven" to accept the promises of God? By faith we have the opportunity of a heavenly life on this earth. The right now! Not just the hereafter.

Here is a serious thought! There is a story of a lady planning to move to a new town. As she talked with a realtor about houses she became anxious about the neighborhood. So as she asked the realtor about the neighbors and the people near by, the wise realtor after a little thought replied, "what were the people like where you live now?" Her reply was just as the realtor expected, they were rude, hateful and a lot of bother. The realtor's reply was "that's the way they will be here too".

Will our life on this earth be repeated in heaven?

Think about it!

I have just been informed that both arteries in the left side of my neck are totally blocked and not repairable and I am still alive. God is surely amazing.

I wish I could add a romantic end to this story but it has been romantic for 81 years so what more could I ask?

God bless you all.

Copies of this book can be ordered from *lulu.com* on the web.